PROCEEDINGS

OF THE

ANTI-SABBATH CONVENTION,

HELD IN THE MELODEON,

MARCH 23D AND 24TH,

[REPORTED BY HENRY M. PARKHURST.]

KENNIKAT PRESS
Port Washington, N. Y./London

KENNIKAT PRESS SCHOLARLY REPRINTS

Dr. Ralph Adams Brown, Senior Editor

Series on
LITERARY AMERICA IN THE NINETEENTH CENTURY
Under the General Editorial Supervision of
Dr. Walter Harding
University Professor, State University of New York

PROCEEDINGS OF THE ANTI-SABBATH
CONVENTION, HELD IN THE MELODEON

First published in 1848
Reissued in 1971 by Kennikat Press
Library of Congress Catalog Card No: 79-122662
ISBN 0-8046-1311-7

Manufactured by Taylor Publishing Company   Dallas, Texas

ANTI-SABBATH CONVENTION.

TO THE FRIENDS OF CIVIL AND RELIGIOUS LIBERTY:

The right of every man to worship God according to the dictates of his own conscience is inherent, inalienable, self-evident. Yet it is notorious, that in all the States, excepting Louisiana, there are laws enforcing the religious observance of the FIRST DAY OF THE WEEK as THE SABBATH, and punishing as criminals such as attempt to pursue their usual avocations on that day,—avocations which even Sabbatarians recognize as innocent and laudable on all other days. It is true, some exceptions are made to the rigorous operation of these laws, in favor of the Seventh Day Baptists, Jews, and others who keep the seventh day of the week as the Sabbath; but this freedom is granted in condescension to the scruples of particular sects, as a privilege, and not recognised as a natural right. For those, (and the number is large and steadily increasing,) who believe that the Sabbath was exclusively a Jewish institution,—' a shadow of good things to come,' which vanished eighteen hundred years ago before the light of the Christian Dispensation, and therefore that it constitutes no part of Christianity,—*there is no exemption from the penalty of the law;* but, should they venture to labor even for bread on that day, or be guilty of what is called ' Sabbath desecration,' they are liable either to fine or imprisonment! Cases of this kind have occurred in Massachusetts, Vermont, Pennsylvania, and Ohio, within a comparatively short period, where conscientious and upright persons have been thrust into prison, for an act no more intrinsically heinous than that of gathering in a crop of hay, or selling moral or philanthropic publications. There is, therefore, no liberty of conscience allowed to the people of this country, *under the laws thereof*, in regard to the observance of a Sabbath day.

In addition to these startling facts, within the last five years a religious combination has been formed in this land, styling itself 'THE AMERICAN AND FOREIGN SABBATH UNION,' whose specific object it is to impose the Sabbatical yoke yet more heavily on the necks of the American people. In a recent appeal made for pecuniary assistance by the Executive Committee of that Union, it is stated that 'the Secretary (Rev. Dr. Edwards) has visited twenty of the United States, and travelled more than thirty thousand miles, addressing public bodies of all descriptions, and presenting reasons why, as a nation, we should keep the Sabbath—all secular business, travelling and amusement be confined to six days in a week—and all people assemble on the Sabbath, and worship God.' A 'permanent (?) Sabbath document' has been prepared by the Secretary; and 'what has already been done will put a copy of this document into more than three hundred thousand families.' Still greater efforts are to be made by the 'Union' for the furtherance of its object.

That this combination is animated by the spirit of religious bigotry and ecclesiastical tyranny—the spirit which banished the Baptists from Massachusetts, and subjected the Quakers to imprisonment and death, in the early settlement of this country—admits of little doubt. It is managed and sustained by the same spirit which has secured the enactment of penal laws against Sabbath-breaking, (all that the genius of the age will allow,) and the disposition of the combination manifestly is, if they can increase their power, to obtain the passage of yet more stringent laws against those who do not 'esteem one day above another,' but esteem 'every day'—who are not willing that any man shall judge them 'in respect to a holy day, or the new moon, *or the Sabbath*'—and who mean to 'stand fast in the liberty wherewith Christ hath made them free, and not to be entangled again with the yoke of bondage.' Its supporters do not rely solely upon reason, argument, persuasion, but also upon brute force—upon penal law; and thus, in seeking to crush by violence the rights of conscience, and religious liberty and equality, their real spirit is revealed as at war with the genius of republicanism, and the spirit of Christianity.

Believing that the efforts of this 'Sabbath Union' ought to be baffled by at least a corresponding energy on the part of the friends of civil and religious liberty; —

That the Sabbath, according to the Jewish Scriptures, was given to 'the children of Israel,'—AND TO NO OTHER PEOPLE,— as 'a sign' between them and God, and terminated, with all the other Mosaic rituals belonging to the 'ministration of death, WRITTEN AND ENGRAVEN IN STONES,' on the introduction of 'THE MINISTRATION OF THE SPIRIT,' and the substitution of 'A BETTER COVENANT, which was established upon better promises'; —

That Christianity knows nothing of a holy day, but only of a holy life,—the possession of a spirit which works no ill to any one, and is 'THE FULFILLING OF THE LAW'; —

That the worship of God does not pertain to any particular day—is not a special, isolated performance—and cannot 'come by observation'—but is purely spiritual in its nature, and comprehended in a cheerful obedience to the will of the Father, as far as it is made known; —

That the distinction made between sacred and secular acts, by the advocates of Sabbath keeping,—the *sacred* being the strict performance of religious observances, and the *secular* such as undoing heavy burdens, letting the oppressed go free, reclaiming the drunkard, laboring in the field or in the workshop, public travelling, transporting the United States mail,— is a distinction not based upon reason or Christianity, but calculated to lower the tone of individual and public morality, and to depress the immutable standard of moral obligation; —

That the Sabbath, as now recognized and enforced, is one

1*

of the main pillars of Priestcraft and Superstition, and the stronghold of a merely ceremonial Religion; —

That, in the hands of a Sabbatizing clergy, it is a mighty obstacle in the way of all the reforms of the age,—such as Anti-Slavery, Peace, Temperance, Purity, Human Brotherhood, &c. &c.,—and rendered adamantine in its aspect towards bleeding Humanity, whose cause must not be pleaded, but whose cries must be stifled, on its 'sacred' occurrence; — and believing, especially,

That all penal laws respecting the religious observance of any day as the Sabbath are despotic and anti-christian, and ought to be immediately abrogated; —

That the interference of the State, in matters of religious faith and outward observances, is not only unwarrantable, but a usurpation not to be tolerated; —

That they who are for subjecting to pains and penalties, all who do not construe the Scriptures in their light, in regard to a religious observance, are actuated by a mistaken or malevolent spirit, which is utterly at variance with the spirit of Christ, which in various ages has resorted to the dungeon, the rack, the gallows, and the stake, for the accomplishment of its purpose, and which ought to be boldly confronted and rebuked ;—

We, the undersigned, therefore, invite all who agree with us essentially in these views of the Sabbath question, to meet IN CONVENTION, in the city of Boston, on THURSDAY and FRIDAY, the 23d and 24th of March next, to confer together, and to decide upon such measures for the dissemination of light and knowledge, on this subject, as may be deemed expedient.

In publishing this call for an ANTI-SABBATH CONVENTION, we desire to be clearly understood. We have no objection either to the first or the seventh day of the week *as a day of rest from bodily toil*, both for man and beast. On the contrary, *such rest is not only desirable, but indispensable*. Neither man nor beast can long endure unmitigated labor. But we do not believe that it is in harmony with the will of God, or the physical nature of man, that mankind should be doomed to hard and wasting toil six days out of seven, to obtain a bare subsistence. Reduced to such a pitiable condition, the rest of one day in the week is indeed grateful, and must be regarded as a blessing; but it is wholly inadequate to repair the physical injury or the moral degradation consequent on such protracted labor. It is not in accordance with the law of life, that our race should be thus worked, and only thus partially relieved from suffering and a premature death. *They need more*, AND MUST HAVE MORE, *instead of less rest;* and it is only for them to be enlightened and reclaimed—to put away those things which now cause them to grind in the prison-house of Toil, namely, idolatry, priestcraft, sectarism, slavery, war, intemperance, licentiousness, monopoly, and the like—in short to live IN PEACE, obey the eternal law of being, strive for each other's welfare, and 'glorify God in their bodies and spirits which are his'—and they will secure the rest, not only of one day in seven, but of a very large portion of their earthly existence. To them shall be granted the mastery over every day and every hour of time, as against want and affliction; for the earth shall be filled with abundance for all.

Nor do we deny the right of any number of persons to observe a particular day of the week as holy time, by such religious rites and ceremonies as they may deem acceptable to God. To their own master, they stand or fall. In regard to all such matters, it is for every one to be fully persuaded in his own mind, and to obey the promptings of his own conscience; conceding to others the liberty he claims for himself.

The sole and distinct issue that we make is this:—We maintain that the seventh day Sabbath was exclusively Jewish in its origin and design; that no holiness, in any sense, attaches to the first day of the week, more than to any other; and that the attempt to compel the observance of any day as 'THE SABBATH,' especially by penal enactments, is unauthorized by scripture or reason, and a shameful act of imposture and tyranny. We claim for ourselves, and for all mankind, the right to worship God according to the dictates of OUR OWN CONSCIENCES. This right, inherent and inalienable, is cloven down in the United States; and we call upon all who desire to preserve civil and religious liberty to rally for its rescue.

By that infallible test of conscious rectitude which Jesus gave to his disciples,—' Whatsoever ye would that men should do to you, do ye even so to them,'—let those who Sabbatize on the first day of the week be measured. At present, they constitute the majority, we the minority, in this country;— hence, the legislative power is in their hands, which they do not scruple to use for the purpose of binding and coercing our consciences. Now let the case be reversed. Suppose this power were in the hands of those who do not Sabbatize, and they should proceed to enact penal laws, forbidding the observance of any day as the Sabbath—would not the Sabbatarians cry out against such laws as vexatious and tyrannical, destructive of the rights of conscience, and a disgrace to the statute book?

We are aware that we shall inevitably be accused, by the chief priests, scribes and Pharisees of the present time, as was Jesus by the same class in his age, as ' not of God,' because we ' do not keep the Sabbath day '; but we are persuaded, that to expose the popular delusion which prevails on this subject, is *to advance the cause of a pure Christianity, to promote true and acceptable worship, and to inculcate strict moral and religious accountability, in all the concerns of life,* ON ALL DAYS OF THE WEEK ALIKE. If we are ' infidels ' or ' heretics ' for this belief, we are content to stand in the same condemnation, on this point, with TYNDALE, LUTHER, CALVIN, MELANCTHON, ROGER WILLIAMS, JOHN MILTON, PENN, FOX, PRIESTLEY, BELSHAM, PALEY, WHITBY, Archbishop WHATELEY, and a host of others, who are everywhere lauded by the various sects with which they are identified as among the brightest ornaments of the Christian Church, and who are essentially agreed with us in the opinion, that the Sabbath was A JEWISH INSTITUTION.

WM. LLOYD GARRISON, Boston, Mass.
FRANCIS JACKSON,   "   "
THEODORE PARKER,   "   "
EDMUND JACKSON,   "   "

CHARLES F. HOVEY, Boston, Mass.
JOHN W. BROWNE, " "
MARIA W. CHAPMAN, " "
CHARLES K. WHIPPLE, " "
SAMUEL MAY, Jr. " "
ROBERT F. WALLCUT, " "
SAMUEL PHILBRICK, Brookline, Mass.
WILLIAM A. WHITE, Watertown, "
INCREASE S. SMITH, Dorchester, "
EDMUND QUINCY, Dedham, "
LORING MOODY, Lynn, "
ANDREW ROBESON, New Bedford, Mass.
JOSEPH CONGDON, " " "
STEPHEN S. FOSTER, Worcester, "
ABBY KELLEY FOSTER, " "
JOSHUA T. EVERETT, Princeton, "
GEORGE W. BENSON, Northampton, "
PARKER PILLSBURY, Concord, N. H.
LUTHER MELENDY, Amherst, "
JAMES MOTT, Philadelphia, Pa.
LUCRETIA MOTT, " "
EDWARD M. DAVIS, " "
CHARLES C. BURLEIGH, "
HENRY C. WRIGHT, " "
J. MILLER McKIM, " "
WM. LOGAN FISHER, " "
THOMAS McCLINTOCK, Waterloo, N. Y.
JOSEPH C. HATHAWAY, Farmington, "
JOSEPH A. DUGDALE, Selma, Ohio.
SAMUEL BROOKE, Salem, "

MEETING OF THE CONVENTION.

Pursuant to the Call, the Convention convened at the Melodeon, on Thursday, March 23d, at 10 o'clock, A. M. The meeting was called to order by Wm. Lloyd Garrison, who read the Call.

On motion of Francis Jackson, of Boston,

Voted, That a committee of three be appointed to nominate a list of officers for the Convention.

Daniel Ricketson of New Bedford, William Sparrell of Boston, and Nathaniel Spooner of Plymouth, were appointed said committee, who reported the subjoined list, and the persons therein named were duly elected : —

President.
GEORGE W. BENSON, of Northampton.

Vice Presidents.
FRANCIS JACKSON, of Boston ;
EDWARD M. DAVIS, of Philadelphia ;
SAMUEL PHILBRICK, of Brookline ;
EDMUND QUINCY, of Dedham ;
INCREASE S. SMITH, of Dorchester ;
JOSEPH CONGDON, of New Bedford.

Secretaries.
DANIEL RICKETSON, of New Bedford ;
ELIZA J. KENNY, of Salem.

Business Committee.
WM. L. GARRISON, C. C. BURLEIGH, JOHN W. BROWNE, MARIA W. CHAPMAN, LUCRETIA MOTT, HENRY C. WRIGHT, PARKER PILLSBURY.

Treasurer.
ROBERT F. WALLCUT.

The Convention was then addressed, in a few appropriate remarks, by the President; and letters from Samuel Myers, of Ohio, Dr. A. Brooke, and others, were read, which, on motion of Mr. Garrison, were accepted by the Convention, to be published with its doings.

The following resolutions were then offered by Mr. Garrison, for the consideration of the Convention: —

1. *Resolved*, That they who are for subjecting to fine or imprisonment, such as do not receive their interpretation of the Scriptures, in regard to the observance of the first day of the week as the Sabbath, are actuated by a mistaken or malevolent spirit, which is utterly at variance with the spirit of Christ —which, in various ages, has resorted to the dungeon, the rack, the gallows and the stake, for the accomplishment of its purpose,—and which ought to be boldly confronted and rebuked.

2. *Resolved*, That the penal enactments of the State Legislature, compelling the observance of the first day of the week as the Sabbath, are despotic, unconstitutional, and ought to be immediately abrogated; and that the interference of the State, in matters of religious faith and ceremonies, is a usurpation which cannot be justified.

3. *Resolved*, That as conflicting views prevail in the community, which are cherished with equal sincerity, respecting the holiness of days, and as it is the right of every class of citizens to be protected in the enjoyment of their religious sentiments on this and every other subject pertaining to the worship of God, all classes should be united in demanding a repeal of the enactments alluded to, on the ground of impartial justice and Christian charity.

4. *Resolved*, That this Convention recommends to all the friends of religious liberty throughout the country, the presentation of petitions to the next Legislature, in every State in which such laws exist, praying for their immediate repeal, and protesting against their enactment, as an unhallowed union of Church and State.

5. *Resolved*, That if the Legislature may rightfully determine

the *day* on which the people shall abstain from labor for religious purposes, it may also determine the *place* in which they shall assemble, the *rites* and *ordinances* which they shall observe, the *doctrines* which they shall hear, the *teachers* which they shall have over them, and the peculiar *faith* which they shall embrace; and thus entirely subvert civil and religious freedom, and enable Bigotry and Superstition, as of old, to

> ' Go to their bloody rites again—bring back
> The hall of horrors, and the assessor's pen,
> Recording answers shriek'd upon the rack—
> Smile o'er the gaspings of spine-broken men,
> And perpetrate damnation in their den ! '

6. *Resolved*, That as it has been found safe, politic and beneficial, to allow the people to decide for themselves in all other religious observances, there is no reason to doubt that the same good results would attend their liberation from the bondage of a Sabbatical law ; for ' where the spirit of the Lord is, there is liberty.'

7. *Resolved*, That under the Christian dispensation, it is a Jewish characteristic to talk of sacred days, places, rites and ceremonies ; for these, at their highest value, are only means to an end, to be used, modified or repudiated, according to circumstances—and that end is, the benefit of man : hence, man is the only object that should be regarded as sacred on earth.

8. *Resolved*, That as it is a sound rule of law, which excludes the testimony of one who is directly and strongly interested in a case on trial; so it is equally just, when a Sabbatical institution is before the Court of Reason for adjudication, to rule out the declarations of a body of men in regard to it, who, filling clerical and priestly offices, depend on its alleged sanctity and rigid observance for their employment, remuneration, influence and power.

9. *Resolved*, That the attempt to frighten the ignorant and unenlightened into a belief, that God frequently suspends the natural laws of the universe, and miraculously interferes to punish with blasting judgments such as engage in labor or re-

creation on the first day of the week—upsetting them in boats on the water, overturning them in vehicles on the land, burning their dwellings and barns, rendering barren and unproductive their farms, visiting with grievous sickness their persons, or smiting them or their cattle to the earth with a bolt from heaven—is either superstitious error or bold effrontery; for it not only expressly contradicts the declaration of Jesus, that God " causeth his sun to rise on the evil and on the good, and sendeth rain on the just and on the unjust "—that we can be " the children of our Father who is in heaven," only by returning good for evil, and blessing for cursing—but it is disproved by universal experience and observation, as such incidents are common to every day of the week alike, and are not in any manner affected by the fact that it is the first, any more than that it is the last day of the week, on which they occur.

10. *Resolved*, That they who resort to such a mode of establishing their Sabbatical assumption, give indubitable proof that they are either grossly superstitious, or designedly fraudulent; straining at a gnat, and swallowing a camel—or, for a pretence, making long prayers, and devouring widows' houses.

11. *Resolved*, That as it is not pretended that such extraordinary and special judgments attend the violation of the other commands in the Decalogue, it follows, according to the logic of the Sabbatarians, that the fourth commandment is of more value than the other nine; so that, in the sight of God, it is incomparably more offensive to indulge in work or recreation on the Sabbath, than it is to worship idols, to dishonor father and mother, to lie, steal, commit adultery, and murder!

12. *Resolved*, That as the duty of observing the first day of the week is not enjoined either in the second chapter of Genesis, or the twentieth chapter of Exodus, or in any other portion of the Old Testament, any reference to the Jewish scriptures, in support of such observance, is not only impertinent, but condemnatory of the present general practice; for the old Hebrew injunction runs:—" The *seventh* day is the Sabbath."

13. *Resolved*, That the proscriptive spirit of modern Sabbatarians is the more severely to be censured, inasmuch as not

an intimation is to be found in the New Testament, that the first day of the week is to be regarded as the Sabbath, instead of the seventh: nor is Sabbath-breaking, whether relating to the first or seventh day, in any instance recognized or reproved by Christ or his Apostles as a sin, nor do they inculcate any principle involving such recognition or reproof.

14. *Resolved*, That the design of the American Church, in its present strenuous efforts for the Sabbatical observance of the first day of the week, is obviously for a show of piety, and to withdraw public attention from its corruption and guilt as pertaining to "the weightier matters of the law, judgment, mercy and faith."

15. *Resolved*, That in the sudden zeal of the Free Church of Scotland, in behalf of the Sabbath, the same artifice is apparent, on the part of that Church, to divert attention from its profligate fellowship with the man-stealing churches in the southern portion of the United States, they having given to its "sustentation fund" the price of blood, in return for its religious sanction.

16. *Resolved*, That it is perfectly in character for those religious bodies, on both sides of the Atlantic, who care nothing for the desecration of *man*, to be deeply concerned for the sanctity of a *day*.

17. *Resolved*, That a Sabbatizing clergy, in resisting, as far as practicable, every great reformatory movement,—and in protesting against the advocacy of the cause of the slave, of peace, of temperance, of labor, of human brotherhood, on the first day of the week, as a desecration of the day, and injurious to the interests of religion,—have revealed themselves in their true character as "wolves in sheep's clothing," and done more to bring their "holy day" into contempt than any other class of men.

18. *Resolved*, That it is not only lawful, but morally obligatory, to do well on every day of the week; and that no day is too holy to plead the cause of suffering humanity, to seek health for the body and recreation for the mind, to engage in useful employment, to promote the arts and sciences, to travel on railways or in any other manner, according to the necessi-

ties, inclinations or tastes of individuals, in the spirit of Christian liberty.

Whereas, the innocence or criminality of any act is not to be determined by the day on which it is performed, but depends upon its intrinsic character, and the motives with which it is done; and whereas, whatever it is right to do on one day, it is right to do on any day; therefore,

19. *Resolved,* That it is as innocent an act to plough in the field, to fish on the sea, to work in the shop, to ride in the railroad car, to indulge in recreation and amusement, on the first as on any other day of the week.

20. *Resolved,* That with the observance of the first day of the week simply as a day of bodily rest, in the present deplorable condition of the laboring classes, we have no controversy; on the contrary, we regard it as an indispensable relaxation, both for men and animals who are severely taxed six days out of seven; but we deny that this excessive toil and imperfect rest are in accordance with physiological law, or the design of the universal Father in the creation of man, or that they are the highest attainable state of the human race — and we would remove from the minds of all, every superstitious notion as to the peculiar sanctity of the day.

The following resolution, offered by Mr. Garrison, was adopted :

That all persons who agree in the sentiments expressed in the Call for this Convention, and who regard all days as alike sacred, shall be considered members of this Convention.

On motion of C. C. Burleigh, the second resolution, relating to the penal laws enforcing the Sabbatical observance of the first day of the week, was taken up for discussion.

Mr. Burleigh then proceeded to address the Convention, as follows :—

As it seems hardly desirable that we should be waiting for each other, I will introduce to the attention of the audience one of the resolutions which have been laid upon the table, and which I suppose are, of course, subject to be called up at any moment, and will make it the text of a few remarks. It is that which points directly to the prominent object of our assembling — the second of the series:

Resolved, That the penal enactments of the State Legislature, compelling the observance of the first day of the week as the Sabbath, are despotic, unconstitutional, and ought to be immediately abrogated; and that the interference of the State, in matters of religious faith and ceremonies, is a usurpation which cannot be justified.

As we have, in the Call which has been read this morning, announced our perfect willingness that every man should keep what day of the week he pleases, and should keep it in such a manner as he believes to be right; as we have announced that it is not our desire to interfere with any man's religious faith, or corresponding practice; we ask only, that the same right should be allowed to us, that we concede to others. We only claim, that what we believe to be our duty, we may do without molestation. If we believe that the law of God, written upon the constitution of our nature, *requires,* not simply permits, that we should, on each of the seven days of the week, devote a certain portion of the time to physical exertion — to that exercise which will promote the health of the body, and a certain portion of it to that rest of the soul which is needful to repair the waste of our energies — we claim the right to work, without being exposed to the penalties of human enactments. We claim the right to rest, whether it be the first day or the seventh day of the week, without having enforced upon us the exposition of the divine law which is to be found in some of the publications of Sabbatical Societies, teaching that, during six days, we must continue in our secular employments, inasmuch as the command as strongly enjoins six days labor as the seventh day's rest.

We ask to be left free to exercise our own judgments, to obey our own consciences, in this matter. We believe the only Lawgiver, whose authority is supreme above us, is God. We believe that the only Court, whose interpretations of the law we are to receive without question, and to obey without hesitation, is conscience. And, therefore, when conscience has interpreted to us the requirements of the divine law, we protest against the interference of another tribunal in the requirement of an action which God's law, under the interpretation of our consciences, forbids. Here, we think, we stand upon the broad ground of natural right. We think that, let the Constitution be what it may, let the statute be what it may, let judicial precedent be what it may, we have a right, by reason of our human nature, by reason of our equal human nature with all other men, to claim and exercise this liberty of conscience.

Moreover, we not only claim that this is our right, but we affirm that it is our duty; we affirm that, as true liege subjects of the King of Heaven, we have no right to submit our consciences to the control of our fellow-subjects in this matter. To admit of control in this matter, is to be guilty of high treason against the sovereignty of Heaven. We have no more right to do it, than the lieges of Queen Victoria have a right to acknowledge the authority of one another to reverse an Act of Parliament, or to require conduct contrary to the established law of the land. Infinitely stronger, indeed, is the contrast, in the present case, than in that which, for the sake of illustration, I have for a moment cited. It is our duty always to do that which we believe God enjoins. We may not say that we will do that duty, subject to the will and pleasure of our representatives in General Court assembled. To my mind, nothing is clearer than that the absolute right of a free conscience grows necessarily out of the truth, that we owe obedience to God alone, in this universe. That no other being has the right to control us, is necessarily the result of the proposition, that this one Being has the right. There can be no concurrent jurisdiction, where there is not absolute certainty of concurrent judgments, concurrent desires and wills. If, then, your will absolutely concurs with God's will, — and if your representation of that will to me absolutely concurs with the representation which my conscience makes of God's will to me, — then it matters not whether you claim legislative power over me; for it is only claiming that I shall do what I think is right to do without the statute.

2*

If, on the other hand, your will conflicts with my sense of right, — if the will the legislature has set forth is not the same as the will of God as conscience represents it to me, — then I must choose between the two: I must do that which I believe God requires, or I must do that which you require, though I believe God forbids it. Now, which must I do? I put it to your common sense, to your natural instinct; which must I do? Which will you do? A friend very solemnly admonished me not to be present at this Convention, not to be seconding the evil machinations of him who was here, addressing the people, from week to week. I asked him, whether I was to be guided by his convictions of duty, or by mine. Sometimes, he said, men are mistaken in their convictions of duty; they think that to be right, which in reality is wrong. But, said I, thinking as I do, which must I do, — that which I think God requires, or that which I think God forbids; that which I believe is right, or that which I believe is wrong? But you may think it is right, and yet it is not right, said he. Must I then do what I believe to be wrong? No, he could not say that I must do that; as if I could avoid doing either one or the other; but, really, I do not see any road between the two. He said that I must not do wrong, though he was not quite ready to admit that I might do what I believed to be right; as if the keenest and most delicate edge of metaphysics could anywhere slip in between the two to find a joint. The case, to my mind, is perfectly clear. I must either renounce my allegiance to God, or I must maintain my absolute right to a free conscience.

But it is said, You must exercise your rights in due subordination to the respective rights of your neighbors. If you believe that one day is just as good as another, still you must not infringe the right of another man to worship God, without molestation or distraction from your secular callings. You must not go into the field or the workshop, because it is offensive to his feelings. Well, if you will appeal to me on this ground, on the ground of my yielding my admitted right on account of the prejudices and feelings of my neighbors and friends, I will entertain the appeal, and consider how far I can consistently, in regard to the principle involved, pay that deference. I do not insist upon it, that I am bound always to exercise the rights which I have. I have the right to do many things, which I am willing not to do at certain times. But when my *right* is questioned, it seems to me that the question takes a somewhat different aspect. When you come to me, and say that it is lawful for the legislature of the land to forbid me to do anything which will offend the prejudices of my neighbors, the legislature having no right to do this, I shall protest against the enactment of such a statute. I shall demand its repeal, if enacted, and demand it both upon the ground of my *natural* rights, and upon the ground of the unconstitutionality of this kind of legislation over us. The Constitution having guarantied to us the right of conscience, they have no power to confer privileges, or to impose penalties or restrictions upon any man, or any class of men, on account of their opinions. Is it constitutional to forbid, under pains and penalties, fine or imprisonment, what I believe God requires at my hand, or permits me to do? If I think it my right, or perhaps even my duty, to go into my office or shop, the legislature says, " You shall not do it." I come forward, and plead conscience. The legislature tramples my appeal to the dust. Has it any right to do so?

There is brought up what may be termed the " police argument"; that we must have some regulations to preserve good order in society. You must consent to forego your rights, in this particular, it is said; you must surrender your conscience, for the sake of peace, for the sake of the quiet of places of religious worship. But which of us must do that? Why must you ask me to yield more than yourselves? Paul's doctrine was, " We that are strong ought to bear the infirmities of the weak." You who are confident in your strength, you who are the majority, who have the public sentiment, who have the education of the thoughts, and the habits growing for centuries in the multitudes, who have the superstition on your side, can you not bear our infirmity, so as to let us have the

peculiar privilege, if anybody must have it? Oh, no, the
majority must rule! Shall the majority rule in matters of conscience? Can you count consciences? Can you count moral
principles? Can you count the impulses of the heart, the faculties of the soul, the multitudinous cords that bind the
individual to the universal heart? If you can, you may
count majorities in cases of conscience. I am the majority, and
you are the majority, in every question of conscience. I am
the majority, when the question is to be decided concerning
my conscience; you are the majority, when it is concerning
yours. Can you speak of ballots and ballot boxes, of the ayes
and noes of the legislative hall, against this right of individual
conscience? It stands too high for legislative power to reach
up to it.

, But I must come back to the question of mere favor, a yielding in deference to the feelings and prejudices of our fellow-
men. The legislature has no right to meddle with that; it has
no right to enforce what are sometimes called " the imperfect"
moral duties of kindness and civility. I have a right to put on
my hat when I walk into your parlor, and sit down there.
Though the laws of etiquette may require me to take it off,
what is that to me? In obedience to that, and to another law,
I should probably take off my hat, on going into your house;
but has the legislature a right to require it? If you go into
the Catholic Church, and attempt to wear your hat, you will
probably have it removed by the officers of the church. Our
troops in Mexico were made to uncover their heads, and bend
their knees, before the elevated host, in conformity to Catholic
prejudices; and the very men and the very religious presses
which are the loudest in advocacy of the Sabbath regulations,
were equally loud in condemnation of that act, as gross idolatry on the part of our soldiers, and as rank despotism, which
it is vain to attempt to justify by any of the laws of military
discipline, on the part of the generals. If, then, even military
discipline cannot justify it; if the prejudices of the surrounding
multitudes, and that, too, when the reasons for the policy were
so strong as in the case referred to, could not justify that

requirement, how much less can your free Constitution authorize civil legislation to enforce Sabbatical observances on the
people, on the ground of deference to prejudices, or on any
other ground you choose to put it on!

If we fall back from this ground, then, of mere deference,
the question arises, what right has anybody to make a prefer-
ence between the Jew and Seventh Day Baptist, and the First
Day worshipper, and those who esteem every day alike? If I
have as good a right to be protected in my worship as you in
yours, we will suppose I am a Jew. I am compelled, by your
law, to rest on the first day of the week. My working disturbs
your meditation; not that I make a clamor, which interrupts
the preaching you wish to hear, or the prayer in which you
wish to join; for I may be in the next street, or half a mile, or
two miles from your meeting-house; but because the mere
knowledge of my act of desecration of this day is troublesome
to you, and prevents your exercising your devotional feelings
as you wish to exercise them. Therefore, you say, it is right
to forbid my working on the first day of the week. My devotional feelings should be respected as much as yours; and now
I want you to lie by on the seventh day of the week, that I may
worship in quiet. Then come up our Quaker brethren, who
have two Sundays in every week; rather, they have seven
Sundays in every week, but they have two days of public
assembling for religious worship. They say, "We come together on first day, and get along very well, because everybody
is still; but on fourth day or fifth day, we find the carriages
rattling along the streets, we hear the hammers busy in the
shops, we see the ploughs driving through the soil in the
fields, and we are continually annoyed and molested. We
have as good a right as you to be quiet. We have as good a
right to be free from this continual din of secular employments
on our days of religious worship; and you must therefore make
a law, that, as our days of meeting are sometimes fourth day,
and sometimes fifth day, there shall be no secular employments
on either of these days." Then in come some of our newly-
arrived citizens from Tunis or Constantinople, where they have

lately abolished their slave markets and slavery, eager to sit
down amidst a free people, *where slavery was never known or
tolerated,*—eager to enjoy our free institutions, and our liberty
of conscience. They worship on Friday, and it is a great
annoyance to them, when they turn their faces towards Mecca,
and say, "God is God, and Mahomet is his prophet," to have
somebody driving between them and the object of their gaze,
with his merchandize or his load of wood. They don't like to
see the shops open on that day; and so you must forbid all
work on the sixth day of the week. Then we have Sundays
from Wednesday morning, not ending till Sunday night; and
if we will examine closely, there may be some, and if anywhere, it might be so here, where the oppressed of all other
nations come for refuge, who worship on Monday or Tuesday,
and they must be accommodated; and so the best way is to
declare all secular employments to be wrong, and to punish
them by imprisonment or fine, on any day of the seven—and
we shall then have a paradise of fools in good earnest.

I see but one escape from this absurdity, with anything like
harmony with present legislation, and that is, to say that, however valuable conscience is, in itself, it must be surrendered, to
gratify the feelings of the majority. How large a majority wish
for this? There are a great many, who do not wish a law
restraining the individual rights on this subject, but who, at
the same time, do not care much about it, and acquiesce in the
present laws. They do not care enough about it to change the
existing laws, but would rather prefer no prohibition. Have
you a right to count them as a part of your majority? I know
it is generally done. Therefore I think it is, that we have a
right to make an appeal to the great body of the people, and
show them the reasonableness of our demand. Besides, when-
ever you take this ground, you are pushing your Sabbath argument against the rocks on the other shore. If you escape
unconstitutional legislation, if you admit the right of the majority to prescribe a day of rest, or for religious worship, then, if
the party holding the majority should wish the seventh, sixth,
fifth, fourth, third, or second day, it has a right to prescribe

that; and then all the sanctity of the Sabbath is gone. It is a mere political religion. Political majorities are made, forsooth, the commentators upon God's law, and are to prescribe what day is sacred, and what day is secular!

But, we are told, "Oh, you are only required to abstain from work on the first day of the week; you may worship when you please. We do not infringe on your right of conscience; you may *worship* just as you will, on the seventh day, the fifth day, or the fourth day; but on the first day, we require you not to *work*. You need not come to our meeting-house, to engage in our worship; you may worship at your own time and place, and we do not impose any penalty at all upon you for that." Indeed! suppose that I entertain opinions differing from yours; and now I say to you, that if you will not conform to my notions, if you will not come where I think you ought, and listen to the sermon and the prayer, then I shall require of you to pay the penalty of the wages of ten days in every year. That is the fine that I impose upon you, and you protest that it is wicked and unconstitutional, and that it is contrary to the rights of conscience. And so you turn round, and make me pay the wages of fifty-two days' labor in every year, and call it perfectly right. The Jew, who is compelled to lie by on the first day of the week, is losing one-sixth part of the entire working period of his existence. So, too, with the Seventh Day Baptist; he loses one-sixth part of his whole working time. You demand, not a tithe, but a sixth part of his substance,—for what is his substance but the result of his labor? To demand that one-sixth part of his time shall be sacrificed, is the same as to say that one-sixth part of his earnings, of his income, of his property, of his means of subsistence and usefulness, shall be sacrificed;—a pretty heavy tax, I think, upon difference of religious opinion. In the case of the man who believes all days alike, it amounts to not quite so large a proportion, although the same amount of actual time; it amounts to one-seventh, instead of one-sixth. Or it *may* be one-sixth of *his* time, too. He may think that the law of distribution is not four meals to-day, and two to-morrow—or six to-day, and none to-morrow. It may be that he thinks we ought to distribute our labor and rest over all the days of the week, as we distribute our taking of food. He may think that to take twenty-four consecutive hours of rest is as unnatural as to take six consecutive meals in one day; and that it is as unreasonable to go six days without the usual rest, as to go all one day without the usual nourishment. He may be in the wrong, but he is sincere in it. In obedience to his law, therefore, he will abstain from bodily activity in each one of the seven days; and, of course, he too loses a sixth part of the time, or even more than that, if he believes a larger proportion of the time is necessary for rest.

In fact, this Sabbatical institution imposes upon the majority, who do not agree with its principles, a very heavy pecuniary fine, to say nothing of the infringement upon their principles. We denounce such legislation, therefore, as both despotic and unconstitutional. We denounce it, even if you assume the perfect truth and justice of the opinions upon which it is based, as to the first day of the week. The question, whether one day is more sacred than another, will come up in another resolution, and I intend to confine myself to the hurtfulness of prescribing rules and regulations concerning any day of the week.

But, in some of the States, they make a discrimination between certain classes of dissentients from the popular faith, and certain other classes. They say, "We will allow you to rest on the seventh day of the week, and to work on the first day, if, indeed, such are your conscientious convictions upon the time of the Sabbath." So the laws are made in New Jersey, and perhaps in some other States, discriminating between the Seventh Day Baptists and others; permitting them, and I suppose the Jews will be included, but forbidding others, to labor on the first day. You have observed your Sabbath, they say, and therefore you have a right to work on our Sabbath, or day of rest. First, that fails to come up to the ground of right. We say, you have no more right to confer the privilege upon the Jew, or the Seventh Day Baptist, than upon the first day Baptist. You have no right to confer such privileges upon anybody. It is undoubtedly a compromise; and yet it is the compromise which wrong is always ready to make to right,—a compromise in detail, while the principle is tenaciously held. But, secondly, that strikes the argument of deference entirely aside. They say, we must not annoy the first day worshippers; and yet, if we will only worship on the seventh day, we may annoy them as much as we please. If we will only agree to be idle one day of the week, they don't care which day it is. Is there not rank absurdity in that kind of reasoning, if reasoning it can be called? Does it not show that the argument has no foundation but in prejudice and in bigotry?

For these reasons, we condemn all Sabbatical legislation; for these reasons, we ask its abrogation.

Mr. Garrison next addressed the Convention, as follows:—

Of all the assumptions on the part of legislative bodies, that of interfering between a man's conscience and his God is the most insupportable, and the most inexcusable. For what purpose do we elect men to go to the General Court? Is it to be our lawgivers on religious matters? Shall we ask of that body when we may work, how we may work, or where we may work? Is it a part of its constitutional power and prerogative to determine that point for us? This passing a law, forbidding me or you to do on a particular day, what is in itself right, on the ground that that day, in the judgment of those who make the enactment, is more holy than another; this exercise of power, I affirm, is nothing better than sheer usurpation. It is the spirit which in all ages has persecuted those who have been loyal to God and their consciences. It is a war upon conscience, and no religious conclave or political assembly ever yet carried on that war successfully to the end. You cannot, by any enactments, bind the consciences of men, nor force men into obedience to what God requires.

Who wants to be persecuted on account of his own conscientious views? I will ask the first day Sabbatarian—do you claim a right to entertain your views, without molestation, in regard to the holiness of time? Most assuredly. How do you make it out that the first day of the week is the Sabbath? "I believe it to be so; and if it is not, to my own Master I stand or fall. Under a government which avowedly tolerates all beliefs, I claim the right, as a first day Sabbatarian, to keep that day as a Sabbath." Well, I do not assail that right. I claim the right also to have my own views of the day; the right to sanctify the first, second, or third, or all days, as I think proper. Now I turn to that first day Sabbatarian, and ask him how he dares to assume infallible judgment against my belief; how he dares to dictate to me to keep the day which he regards as holy, and to say, "If you do not obey me, I will put my hands into your pocket, and take out as much as I please in the shape of a fine; or if I find nothing there, I will put you in prison; or if you resist enough to require it, I will shoot you dead?" How dare he do this? If he is not a ruffian, is he a Christian? Talk of the spirit of justice animating the bosom of the man who comes like a highwayman with, "Do, or *die!*" Who made him a ruler over other men's consciences? In a government which is based on equality, we must have equal rights. No men, however sincere, are to wield forceful authority over others who dissent from them, in regard to religious faith and observance. The case is so plain, that it does not need an argument; and I am confident that, in the course of a few years, there will not be a Sabbatical enactment left unrepealed in the United States, if in any part of Christendom. It belongs to the tyrannical legislation which formerly sent men to the stake, in the name of God and for his glory, because they did not agree in the theological views of those who burnt them to ashes.

In this country, one pharisaical restriction after another, imposed by legislation, has been erased from the statute book, in the progress of religious freedom. We now come to this Sabbatical observance, as the last, perhaps,—a powerful one at any rate. If the Sabbath day be of God, it does not need legislation to uphold it. There is no power which can prevail against it. If it is founded in the nature of man, and in the wants of animals,—as its advocates declare,—then, of course, nature will triumph, and the Sabbath is safe. On the other hand, if it be merely a human contrivance, imposed upon us artfully, in the name of Christ, though of Jewish origin, it is for you and me, if we profess to be followers of Christ, or lovers of freedom, to speak the truth in regard to it, and deny that it has any special claim to religious veneration.

Why should we attempt to legislate upon a question of this kind? Observe how many differences of opinion prevail, honestly and sincerely, in the world, respecting it! Does any one doubt that the Seventh Day Baptists are sincere? Are they not honest, courageous, self-sacrificing men, those who stand out against the law and public sentiment, for conscience' sake? The men, even though they err, who are true to their consciences, cost what it may, are, after all, those who are ever nearest to the kingdom of God. They desire only to know what is right, and they have the spirit in them to do what is right. The great mass of first day Sabbatarians—do they not claim to be conscientious and sincere? And the Quakers, who regard no day as in itself, or by divine appointment, more holy than another,—who will question their honesty or sincerity in this matter? Here, then, are widely conflicting sentiments; but which of these parties shall resort to the arm of violence to enforce uniformity of opinion? The case is easily settled by making it our own, my friends. It is, as truly stated in the Call, based upon the declaration of Jesus, "Whatsoever ye would that men should do to you, do ye even so to them." Now there is no Seventh Day Baptist, who would wish to be proscribed for his views, of course. There is no first day Sabbatarian, who wishes a majority to get into the Legislature to pass laws against the observance of the first day of the week as the Sabbath, or who would not vehemently protest against it. "Whatsoever ye would that men should do to you, do ye even so to them," and the religionist who is not prepared for this, is to be associated with the Scribes and Pharisees of a persecuting age. He is one who joins in the crucifixion of Jesus as a blasphemer.

In this country, we tolerate all religions, but must not tolerate all views with regard to a holy day! Why not? If we tolerate the greater, why not the less? We had better begin at the beginning. Let us tolerate none but the true religion, and no other worship than that of a triune God. Let us have no Jews, no Idolators, no Catholics! We are Protestants; we are evangelical; ours is the true God, ours the true religion; and it is all-important for the welfare of the world, that the true religion should be promoted. Therefore, be it enacted by the Legislature, that only the Protestant religion, in its evangelical form, be allowed on the American soil!

But we do not do this. It is not a crime, in the eye of the law, for a man to make as many idols as he chooses, and to worship them. It is not a crime, in the eye of the law, to reject the doctrine of the Trinity. Time has been, when it was a capital offence to deny the monstrous dogma of transubstantiation as held by the Church of Rome, and the denial carried the heretic to the stake. We tolerate everything, excepting the opinions of men with regard to the first day of the week! Having very successfully gone thus far, I think we may take the next step, and finish the whole category of religious edicts enforced by penal law. Some of you doubtless remember what a hue-and-cry was raised by the religious press and the clergy, at the proposition to amend that portion of the Constitution of Massachusetts, which required persons to be taxed for the support of public worship somewhere. But the spirit of religious liberty came up, and said, "That is tyranny, and the law ought to be,—ay, must be repealed." What was the response of the evangelical press? "This is an infidel movement! This is an attempt to overthrow Christianity!" And it prophesied that, just as surely as the proposed amendment should be adopted, public worship would be sadly neglected. Well, the Constitution was altered, in this respect, notwithstanding this selfish outcry. Is there less of public worship than formerly? The clergy have never been so well sustained as they now are, and no one now laments the change.

Now, the outcry raised against the repeal of all Sabbatical laws, as an infidel movement, is as absurd, as preposterous, as libellous, as the other; and will be found so when those laws cease to be in force. Tie men up to the idea, that one day is more holy than another, and enforce that idea by the infliction of penalties in case of disobedience, and you may make men religious hypocrites, but never Christians. That experiment was tried, with all exactness and severity, under the Old Dispensation. God has written out that experiment in letters of fire, as it were, which shall never go out until all men shall learn that it is not outward observances which are required, but that spirit of the heart and life which consecrates all things to God and humanity.

What a tremendous outcry was raised in England when Daniel O'Connell, in behalf of plundered Ireland, demanded the passage of the Catholic Emancipation Act by the British Parliament! The Protestant clergy and the Protestant press cried out against it. It will never do, they said; the cause of religion will suffer! Where now is the Catholic test? Gone; its ashes are not to be found; but has any injury followed from its repeal? So with regard to the unrighteous restrictions imposed upon the Jews; they were justified on the ground of Christian vigilance and security! But, during the present session of Parliament, the Jews have been admitted to equal rights with all others; and the Jew in England can now take his position anywhere in the government, as well as the Christian. Does any one suppose Christianity will suffer by this? Christianity, as taught by its founder, does not need any governmental safeguards; its reliance for safety and prosperity is not on the rack or the stake, the dungeon or the gibbet, unjust proscription or brutal supremacy. No — it is the only thing under heaven that is not afraid; it is the only thing that repudiates all such instruments as unholy and sinful.

Take another illustration. There are laws in some of the States, forbidding the man to testify who says, " I am not satisfied that there is a God"; who is what is called an Atheist, and yet in moral character, perhaps, is honest, upright, faithful, as any; who is a good neighbor, a good husband, and a good citizen; but then he does not believe in a God according to the popular belief, and he is therefore judged unworthy to testify. Is not this high-handed tyranny? Yet the religious press and

3*

the pulpit will cry out, if you claim equal privileges for the Atheist and Christian, in matters of testimony. But we shall abolish that proscriptive act ere long. Every man must decide for himself, and no one decide for him, as to the Deity he shall recognise, as to the worship he shall perform. Every man feels that it is his duty to decide for himself on points like these; and the moment any man, or body of men, comes to him, and says, " I am to you God — fall down and worship me" — he is to say to that man, or body of men, " Get thee behind me, Satan!" Let us be careful how we trample on human liberty or human conscience. Said the Apostle, " Every one of us must give account of himself" — not to the Legislature of Massachusetts, not to the Congress of the United States — but " unto God." Let God, then, not man, rule over us.

I hope the recommendation contained in one of the resolutions will sink deep into the hearts of all here, — namely, to petition the several State Legislatures for the abrogation of all Sabbatical laws. Let the first day of the week stand on its own basis, as the second or third day stands, and I am satisfied that it will be much more rationally observed than it is now. Getting rid of our superstition concerning it, we shall use the day in a far more sensible and useful manner than is now done.

It is not profane men, immoral men, who are specially interested in this movement. Far otherwise! They are glad, indeed, of any holiday on which to indulge their animal propensities; but they who go forward in a cause like this, must be reformers in principle, and they will assuredly find the evil in the world not with them, but against them. They will find priestcraft on the one hand, and the rabble on the other, joining in a common persecution. Jesus was crucified, not by the Chief Priests and Scribes and Pharisees alone, but it needed the populace to join with them; and then they could nail him to the cross, as they did, between two thieves, for this among other reasons, that he was not of God, because he did not keep the Sabbath day!

The following series of resolutions was introduced by John W. Browne, of Boston:—

1. *Resolved,* That what we call time is only that portion of eternity, measured by earthly life ; and that, therefore, in God, all days are alike holy, all being alike a part of his eternity.

2. *Resolved,* That the Creator God never rested from his work in the creation, but that he worketh hitherto — his creation being this moment unfinished; that constant creation is the law of his existence, and the manifest mode of his acting in external nature ; and thus, that the theological proposition of the Jewish Sabbath as a commemoration of a resting of the infinite Creator on the seventh day, measured by the revolution of this earth, is an absurdity in the theory of spiritual existence, and an exploded proposition in science, which has explored the facts of the creation.

3. *Resolved,* That a Sabbath on the seventh or on the first day of the week, is no part of the teaching of Jesus, but is alien to his spirit; that the religion of Jesus is the life of the soul, not observances of times or forms; and that in all its appeals, it calls upon man as a sacred free will, through the law of truth, and never as a subject, through the power of government.

4. *Resolved,* That a Sabbath one day in seven is a part of the religion and law of a Jew, and can claim no more observance on the ground of reverence from one who is not a Jew, than the Passover or the Pentecost.

5. *Resolved,* That our Sunday, in its distinction from the other days of the week, is made the successor of the Jewish Sabbath, by an interpolation upon Christianity ; that it is an old piece of Hebrew cloth sewed upon the new garment of Christianity.

6. *Resolved,* That the process of theological reasoning, which sustains a religion of Sunday observance as a part of Christianity, is an error and superstition so gross and slavish, that it is in vain to look for the fruits of a true worship in any person who is subject to it ; and that the common cause of religion and humanity demands a testimony against it from all who

have been delivered from its bondage into the light of liberty.

7. *Resolved,* That all observance of Sunday, as a means of personal holiness, through public worship, or whatsoever other mode, ought to be wholly voluntary, because it claims to be religion, whose essence is belief; and that for a Republican Government to enforce the observance of Sunday by penalties, where the private heart goes not with it, is *to enforce the creed of a majority as an absolute religion.*

8. *Resolved,* That in the matter of our Sunday laws, majorities have undertaken to stand in the place of interpreters for God, and establish a form of religion, in the face of the true idea of a government by the people, and in the face of our American Constitutions, whereby government is made incapable of legislating upon what concerns the private conscience alone.

9. *Resolved,* That we greet Sunday with gladness, as a day of voluntary and habitual rest and recreation for man and beast, and that we would hail with gladness yet another day in seven for that purpose ; or, what would be a higher blessing still to humanity, a Sabbath of rest from labor and business, during a portion of the hours of daylight of every day.

10. *Resolved,* That with the habit of voluntary religious observance on Sunday, however its modes may differ from our thought of a high worship, we can have no controversy — our controversy is with the theological and commanded religion of Sunday, oppressing human liberty.

Mr. Browne remarked, — I should like to say a few words to present the subject as it has lain in my own mind. Sunday was pressed upon my childhood as the theological holy day. My own nature, and all the evidences of my youngest reason, contradicted this, and stood up against the restraint. Yet was I nevertheless obliged to live through years of youth and early manhood, under a confused idea that I could not be good, because I did not believe as others seemed to about it. I lived under the cloud of Mosaic-Christian theology, half condemned within myself, because conscious of the condemnation of others. At last the cloud passed away, and I could stand clear in light about the matter, and justify this infidelity to Sunday observance as faith in an inward religion. All, whose reverence must wait upon the verdict of their reason, are thus obliged to dig in darkness through the dogmas of taught religion, to come at the convictions of personal religion; and then they are at rest from doubt, at home in the Father's universe, everywhere, every moment. I think this has been the experience of all natures, which cannot take prescriptions of doctrine for the cure of their souls. My strife against this Sunday is, that it is the supporting centre of a false theology. A sphere of kindred religious errors organizes about it. Let them go away, and no longer keep us in shadow.

Such is my objection against the legal religious Sunday, while I rejoice at it as a day of habitual rest from labor. I would rather see two such days of rest in the week, than one. I would still rather see one-half the hours of daylight of every day in the life of every person on earth, devoted to sacred rest from bodily labor. I ask for labor more than the guaranty of a ten hours' system. I do not believe that human bodies were made temples of the holy ghost, to labor ten hours on each of six days of every week. I believe these temples were made for another purpose than to be mere instruments of labor. I rejoice, then, in the fact of Sunday as a day of rest, and voluntary worship and improvement; but I resist it as of theological authority, as of government religion; and I can never consent to it, in that sense, in my heart and conscience.

I was moved a good deal just before coming into the convention, this morning, by the receipt of a letter, in the handwriting of a woman:—

To the Convention this day assembled.

GENTLEMEN AND GENTLEWOMEN:—In the behalf of many thousands of my sisters, I appeal to you to pause and reflect, before you remove the strong arm of the law from the day observed as the Sabbath. We, who labor seventeen hours a day for six days, should avarice and fashion and need find it *legal* to compel* us, must do so for seven days. Think of us, with our aching heads, our weary hands, our eyes, with every nerve pierced with a needle's point, our starving children, our tasks harder than the slave's in the rice-fields, and remember that the *Law* is a terror to evil-doers. The good need no law, it is not for them. Leave them the only *sign* that man, yes and woman, have souls as well as bodies. Leave us the *pause* when the wheels of labor stop, or we must die. Do not blot out the promises of a better future.

A Seampstress.

With the wish and aspiration of this letter for sacred rest, I have full sympathy; but I see no such consequences to result from the abolition of the Sunday law, as the writer sees. I see that law to exist as a proposition of false theology and bigoted religion, which comes down upon our souls with the might of power, and says, regard this day as holy, and observe it as a holy day in distinction from other days, or I will punish you as a criminal. I say, then, let the law be struck from the statute book, so far as it compels a religious and theological rest. Then, if that be desirable, let there be a law for the protection of labor, that capital may not work up human bodies into profits and dividends, on the same ground as now the law protects children in factories against work more than ten hours in the day, and requires that they shall have schooling at least three months in a year. Let the law of rest from labor stand upon its true foundation. Let it establish rest-days for the sake of man, and not for the sake of theology and dogmatic religion. It seems to me there is no such danger in the result of our wishes, as is anticipated in this letter. I believe those who come to this convention, are the friends of all working souls and bodies; and that they who uphold the Sunday law, are not they who uphold the idea that laboring man and woman are temples of the holy ghost, and too sacred to be used in life on earth as instruments of toil. I believe that those

---

* The argument of our masters is, if you refuse to comply with our conditions, we will give our work to some one who will, and you may starve.

who find themselves together here, are the friends of humanity, resisting this law because power lays it upon the conscience.

One word as to the practical working of this law. Last Sunday afternoon, as I was walking in Washington street, in this city, I met several fine carriages. These carriages belonged, undoubtedly, to rich citizens of this place. The man servant had been commanded, in the morning, to serve the horses, and prepare the carriage to take the family out to air and exercise, for some hours after the Sunday dinner. Now, this was a palpable violation of the law, as it exists. Yet these very persons, I suppose, declaim against this convention as impious, and as seeking to desecrate God's holy day. I have no doubt, too, that these persons who thus break the law, profess to believe the day sacred, and the law an excellent and salutary one. But upon whom does the law operate? Not upon such persons; not upon persons who break it in the recognized forms of common pleasure and travel; but upon the private conscience of the man who, believing that the slave ought to be free, lectures and sells tracts upon that truth on Sundays; or upon the come-outer, who seeks to make his protestation against tyranny and bigotry effectual, by working upon his farm on Sundays. They who profess to believe in the law, but still transgress it, are not touched by it; but they who in their consciences believe the law to be wrong, and for a testimony transgress it, they are the persons whom it punishes. This is the matter of our every day experience. The facts of prosecutions under the law, as they come to our knowledge now, are so. If you will uphold the law in theory, you may break it in practice; if you testify in its face that it is an abomination, you are punished, not for the sake of the law, but because of your protestantism.

C. C. Burleigh next addressed the Convention, as follows:—

It seems to me that those who object to the course we are pursuing, for fear of its evil influence upon the interests of labor, have taken a very short-sighted view. Just look at the course they are pursuing who oppose us. They are using this idea of the sacredness of the Sabbath, of its peculiar holiness,

and the consequent appropriateness of certain peculiar modes
of spending it, as the one great bar in the way of the progress
of that knowledge and those sentiments which are to break
down the oppressive institutions of the world. If we come to
speak for labor, as represented in the down-trodden slave,
whose rights are the rights of labor everywhere, we are told
that the day when the mass of the people are at leisure to hear
us, the day which alone they have at disposal, is too sacred to
be devoted to pleading the cause of the slave! If we come to
turn the attention of the people against that vice, which, by
debasing the soul and destroying the body, makes the laborer
the easily subjected victim of the higher, or, I should say, aris-
tocratic classes,—if we come to preach Temperance, and urge
upon the people the importance of preserving themselves with
sound minds and sound bodies, that they may be able to maintain their rights, and win the respect of their fellow-men,—we
are told that the Sabbath is too holy to give Temperance lectures upon! When we attempt to speak upon the disorganiz-
ation of society, that chaos which we now behold, we are told
that to preach in favor of the organization of labor is not a
suitable subject for holy time! So, whatever be our cause, if
the object of it is to strike down some hoary institution, based
on error, and crushing human hearts beneath its weight,—if
the object is to open the prison-doors, and let labor go free
from its unjust confinement, — we are told that the day is too
holy for that! It is only religious doctrines which are to be
preached on that day. A man may preach, " Servants, be obedient unto your masters,"—and the day is not too holy for that.
He may preach about the turning of water into wine, and
preach, therefore, in favor of wine, and by fair deduction in
favor of alcoholic drinks,—and the day is not too holy for that.
He may preach to the poor to be content and submissive,—
that they must not utter a word of murmuring or complaint, in
all their sufferings and toil,—and that is no violation of holy
time; and so on to the end of the chapter. Martial armies bow
in worship before the sacramental host, and that you condemn
as idolatry; but you send them out to fight their battles on

the first day of the week—to slaughter fellow-beings on the first day of the week—to subject a distant land, that slavery may spread over it—and the Sabbath is fitting for such things. They may strew the plains with one wide scene of carnage, and that is all holy. There is nothing in that, contrary to the proper discharge of the duties of the first day of the week, if we may judge from the perfect silence, the absolute dumbness of those who rebuke the enterprises we are engaged in, — their absolute silence in regard to this mode of spending holy time. Those who are endeavoring to do away this relic of legislation are, in fact, trying to open a pathway for the advance of those principles, for the progress of those enterprises, whose object is to emancipate labor, to equalize the distribution of the products of human toil, to protect the oppressed from the power of capital, and to teach that reverence for man, above all the accidents and circumstances of life, which alone can insure the elevation of the race, which alone can insure the unfolding of all his powers, and his attainment of the full stature of a perfect man.

Mr. Garrison next took the platform, and said:—

" A Working Woman" asks a great deal of us, when she asks us to uphold a law which violates our consciences — a law which we believe to be equally pernicious and oppressive — because she is apprehensive its repeal will add to the severity of labor, without increasing the remuneration of the laborer. She imagines there is virtue in the law to shield, to some extent, from the lash of extortion, the already overburdened; and therein I think she is greatly mistaken. She claims to be one of the working-classes, who are ground down to the earth by the spirit of exaction, the victims of remorseless speculators; and how very graphic and affecting was her description of their sad condition! Erase from the statute book the present law of the Sabbath, and they will be compelled to toil seven days in the week, for the same compensation now obtained for six days' labor. This is her special objection to our movement. It is one which a selfish priesthood, on both sides of the Atlantic, are urging with great

pertinacity, as though they were greatly concerned for the
rights and interests of the working-classes — as though priestcraft were solicitous for the removal of heavy burdens which
are grievous to be borne, instead of binding them upon the
laboring man's shoulders! I am sorry to hear the victim urge
the specious objection of those who victimize, and who, in all
past ages, have been identified with the extortionate and powerful. It is not true that any such calamity would follow
the abolition of all penal legislation in regard to the Sabbath.
The additional exaction that is dreaded cannot be enforced. If
it could, it would have been long ago, any prohibition in the
Decalogue of Moses, or in the statute book of the Commonwealth, to the contrary notwithstanding! But *it would not pay*
— it would exceed the powers of human endurance to be
worked without cessation. One day in the week, for bodily
rest, is the smallest allowance which poor, burdened, crushed
humanity can get along with, without destruction to all
classes. What do those merciless employers and sordid monopolists, who are endeavoring to coin money out of the very
life-blood of the people, care for the fourth commandment?
They do not care for any of the commandments! And if the
Sabbatical law of the State stood in the way of their selfishness, would they hesitate to obliterate it, from motives of
benevolence? What absurdity! Do you suppose the slave-
holder is led, by any consideration of justice or humanity, to
give his slave a peck of corn a week? No! He allows it
simply because his victim cannot subsist upon a less quantity,
and yet perform the task required of him. He would reduce
the quantity to a pint, if the same results would follow; and if
the slave could be made to subsist upon thin air, he would
give him nothing but that. Such is the spirit by which North-
ern monopolists are animated, in their treatment of the laboring classes.

Ludicrously enough, the Rev. Dr. Edwards, in his "Permanent Sabbath Documents," has resorted to Parliamentary and
other statistics, and to the testimonies of eminent medical men,
in order to prove that those who never cease from severe daily

toil, do not get along as well as those who enjoy the rest of one day in seven! It needed, forsooth, all these statistics and testimonies, to convince mankind of this fact. I know of no anti-Sabbatarian, who has ever denied it. But is it not revolting, does it not excite intense moral indignation in every manly bosom, to hear those who are grinding the faces of the poor continually, and "riding booted and spurred upon their backs by the grace of God," vociferating in the ears of their plundered victims, "The Sabbath is the sheet-anchor of your mortal bark! It is God's gift to you, to serve as a break-water against the encroachments of the waves of extortion! As sure as you give up the holiness of the day, the day is gone, and with it will go the bulwark of your security against perpetual toil!" Out upon these deceivers, who never attempt to remove any of the burdens under which the laboring classes are groaning — who inculcate the heart-breaking doctrine, that all things must remain as we now find them, to the end of the world; the same frightful inequalities in society, the same dreadful necessities afflicting the masses — and yet exclaim, as if inspired by the noble sentiment of gratitude, as if animated by the warmest sympathy toward the millions who are running the gauntlet six days out of the seven to pick up enough to keep body and soul together — "How gracious is the Lord to provide for you a day of rest in the week, in which you can repair your wasted energies, and obtain some respite from toil, and also moral and religious instruction!" Yes, laboring men and laboring women! hold on to this day of rest, not superstitiously, not as a peculiarly holy day, but intelligently and rightfully; but be not satisfied with it, nor believe that it is all your beneficent Creator designs that you shall enjoy. Claim more and take more rest. Put away your vices, your crimes, your sins, which now tax your time and labor so heavily — strike at the exercise of that power, which, by the multiplication of armies and navies, of public plunderers and favored monopolists, is eating up your hard-earned substance, and keeping you in shameful vassalage — seek peace, virtue, knowledge, and true piety — hurl to the dust a false Church, with its hireling priesthood, and an oppressive State, with its swarms of office-seeking vampyres — make your interests harmonious instead of antagonistical — and you shall redeem all days from servile toil, and enjoy a perpetual Sabbath. This is the will of God.

Adjourned to meet at a quarter before 3 o'clock.

———

AFTERNOON SESSION.

Convention met pursuant to adjournment, and was called to order by the President.

Voted, That James N. Buffum, Loring Moody, and Lewis Ford be a Committee on Finance and the Roll.

A letter from Ira Wanzer, of Connecticut, was read by Mr. Garrison.

Resolutions, Nos. 1 and 2 of the series offered by Mr. Garrison, were taken up, and an excellent essay read by John W. Browne, in support of the same.

The Convention was then addressed by Rev. Theodore Parker, of Boston, as follows :—

MR. PRESIDENT, — I did not rise, Sir, for the purpose of making a speech. I have an opportunity of saying often, what I wish to say, respecting this and other matters. There are others here, who should have an opportunity to say what they have to say. I will, therefore, detain the audience but very few minutes, and make but very few points.

The first point that I wish to make is, that the Sunday is a purely human institution; that it was originally established as a day for religious services, purely as a human institution. We all know the theory of the Hebrew Sabbath, and it rests on this assumption — that God created the world in six days of the common length, rested on the seventh day, and commanded men, accordingly, forever to rest on that day.

need not say to this audience, that there are no facts in nature to warrant that assertion. The Jewish law of the Sabbath rested on that theory. God made the world in six days, and rested on the seventh, and was refreshed. Well, the Jewish law came as other laws did. It was a human law ; and being enacted in a rude period of mankind, of human history, being enacted in a great measure by priestly persons, it was enacted in the name of God. The priests who wrote the law, I suppose, understood by the phrase, " Thus saith the Lord," nearly the same as we understand by, " Be it enacted," or " Be it ordained." But, take whatsoever view you may of the Jewish law — suppose it came directly from God — it was designed for the Jews only, and nobody else. Suppose it was divine, and intended for all times, we find in the New Testament that Jesus sets it entirely aside. In the first gospel, it is said that Jesus, in his capacity of Messiah, sets aside the Sabbath day, or, at any rate, violates the fundamental law respecting it, declaring that he is greater than the Sabbath day. In the second gospel, he asserts that the human race are superior to the Sabbath day, and therefore it is set aside. In the fourth gospel, another step is taken, and the theory upon which the Sabbath rests is entirely denied — the theory, that God rested on the seventh day. In the fourth gospel, Jesus is represented as denying that theory. " My Father worketh hitherto," he says, " and I also continue to work." It was, in like manner, set aside by the early Christians ; set aside, I will not say universally at first, because a portion of them clung to Jewish rites and Jewish ideas. Presently, that party became the minority.

The early Christians adopted the first day of the week for reasons often mentioned. One of these is, that it was supposed to be the day when Jesus rose from the dead, and therefore a very fit day for the symbol of the new dispensation, the new religious kingdom which Christ came to establish. Another reason is founded on the mythical story in the book of Genesis, that God created the world in six days, and began the work on the first day. The early Christians, therefore, thought that work was holier than rest, at least divine work, and the day on which God began work was more fitted for religious observance than the day on which he stopped work-

4*

ing. For considerably more than three centuries, there was not any claim made for any divine command for keeping the first day of the week; and the Catholic notion of the Sunday, at the present day, is this — that it is a day set apart by the Church, for the purpose of honoring God. The Catholic maintains that the Church is superior to the Bible, to all books and all laws, to everything on earth. In his creed, the Catholic Church had power to separate one day from the rest for religious observances. It had the power, and it exercised the power by separating the first day of the week. It regarded as equally holy the Passover, (Easter) and the whole period of eight days, formerly observed by the Jews, commemorative of the "Resurrection" of Jesus. Then it set apart the day of Pentecost, and a week then, because that was the anniversary of the "Ascension," and "Inspiration" of the Christians. Then there is a third series — the day when Jesus first *showed himself to the people* — the Epiphany. A fourth period was the anniversary of Christ's birth, or Christmas. All these days are regarded by the Catholic Church at this very time, as equally holy with the Sunday. In addition to these are the anniversaries of the birth of several important saints, which are regarded in the Catholic Church in the same light as the Sunday, — days separated from the common purposes of life; not fast-days, not work-days, not days of sanctimonious longfacedness, but days peculiarly devoted to religion, to society, and to joy.

Sunday, then, has no valid claim to divine authority, according to the common notion; but the religious institution of Sunday was resorted to for this reason — it was found useful to have one day in the week in which men could come together eminently for religious purposes. They came together voluntarily for that purpose, and it was found convenient to have one day in which common work should be laid aside, and in which they could be free from that annoyance and assemble. After a little while, no one can say exactly how long, the Church made some Church rules, that if a man did not observe the Sunday, — that is to say, if he did not come to meeting, — he should be ecclesiastically punished. They considered it inexpedient to work on Sunday, for they thought the day might be devoted to better purposes. They thought it a pity that anybody should absent himself from their meeting, and lose the influence of the wise words and fervent prayers that might there and then be uttered. It was found convenient to have several rest-days in the year. Sundays were not thought to be enough, and so they selected the Passover, Pentecost, Epiphany, Christmas, and various saints' days. The law which my friend [Mr. Browne] read, also watched over Friday, because Friday was observed as a fast day by the early Christians. The authors of those edicts did not do it as a matter of religion, but as a matter of expediency. They made their enactments in the same spirit, in which the law says to the traveller, Keep to the right, instead of keeping to the left; in the same spirit in which it says that over certain bridges upon the Connecticut and other rivers, a man shall only go at a certain pace, lest he should shake them to pieces. On the same principle, the Legislature of Massachusetts regulates the fishery in various rivers, as the Charles River, and Taunton, saying that shad and alewives may only be caught on Thursdays and Fridays, or Tuesdays and Fridays, — the object being to preserve the benefit of the fishery as long as possible, and to give it to the whole community; therefore it is desirable to select some days on which men may fish, and some on which they may not fish. That was the spirit in which the early laws were made, which my friend has read this afternoon.

It is commonly supposed that our New England notion, respecting Sunday, is a very old notion; but it seems to me that that is a very great mistake. I know it is a mistake, and experience, I think, has shown that it is a sad mistake. I do not find that any considerable number of persons ever entertained our New England notions, until less than 300 years ago. About the year 1595, Mr. Bound, an English Puritan, wrote a book respecting the Sabbath, in which he claimed that the Hebrew Sabbath was of divine origin, but maintained that, after the resurrection, the Sabbath, and all the laws respecting the Sabbath, were miraculously transferred to the first day of the week. Therefore, all Christians were bound to observe the first day of the week, just as the Jews were bound to observe their Sabbath. That was regarded by intelligent Churchmen—as it was—as a very great heresy in the church. Religious men said it was a *heresy*, and they said right, because it was an innovation, and there was nothing to warrant it. Political men said it was an *absurdity*, and it was an absurdity. The book was written in the days of fanaticism, when the public were rising against the abominations, and frivolity, and wickedness of the Roman church. Now, the Roman church had not made the best use of the Sunday, by any means. It did not offer enough instruction; it had too much for the senses, as some think. But be that as it may, *it had too little for the soul*, as it seems to me. Men commonly think they are never clear of one wrong till they have got the opposite wrong. So the Puritans, disgusted with the frivolity which they saw in the Romish church—disappointed at finding in the Catholic Sunday, in its freedom and its frolic, so little for the direct nurture of religion—went over to the other extreme, and made Sunday—we all know what they made of the Sunday. That was a time of fanatical reaction against old abuses. Mr. Bound, in his book, represented the fanatical reaction. There is no great danger of resisting a wrong too powerfully, but there is great danger of going over to the opposite wrong, and contending that that wrong is the right. It seems as if it would have been easy to settle down upon the Christian idea of the Sunday at that time, and avoid the error of the Catholics, without committing a new error. But the Puritans did not do so; they did commit a new error, and we are met here to-day to correct that error. I would not commit the same fault that the Puritans did, and go to the opposite extreme. If men are fanatical in their notion of keeping the Sunday, I would not be a fanatic and destroy it; for if men now are driven by the spirit of reaction against the Puritanic idea of the Sunday, and go to the opposite extreme, why all the work must be done over again till it is well done.

But I am wandering a little from what I wish to say now. Half a century before Mr. Bound's time, in the reign of Edward VI., it was found necessary to enact laws for the better observance of *Lent* and other periods of fasting. A statute was made in the year 1548 to prohibit the eating of flesh on those days; the reason of the statute is given—not because fasting is enjoined in the Old Testament, but because "*due and godly abstinence is a mean to virtue,*" and that "fishers *may thereby be set at work—and much flesh shall be saved and increased.*" (2d and 3d Edward VI. c. 19.) The statute was revived in the next reign; but to guard against the notion that fasting or eating fish is a virtue in itself—and "because no manner of person shall misjudge of the intent of this statute"—it is enacted, "that *whosoever shall notify that any eating of fish or forbearing of flesh mentioned therein is of any necessity for the saving of the soul of man, or that it is the service of God, otherwise than as other politic laws are and be ; then such persons shall be punished as spreaders of false news.*" [5th Eliz. c. 5, § 18, 39, 40, in *Hallam.*

Now, if the laws respecting the Sabbath were enacted by the British Parliament in the beginning of the seventeenth century, and if the laws of New England and the United States had had such a preamble as that, stating that it was for the public good and for political considerations that they were passed, and not for religious considerations, then we should have been freed from a monstrous amount of abuse, and a deal of tyranny. It seems to me that the history of the Christian church has shown that it is useful to stop, and lay aside common work, and devote one day to rest, to society, to man's spiritual culture; and by spiritual culture, I mean his religious, moral, and intellectual culture — in short, the cultivation of his whole spiritual nature. It seems to me that it is useful to do this now. But I will not dwell upon that point. A clergyman is not a proper person to testify on that point. I love the Sunday, and I love my profession; but lest I should be unduly biassed in that matter, I will say no more respecting it now.

This I will say, that if even it is a religious duty to separate one day from common purposes, and devote it to religious purposes, it seems to me that the *law* need not trouble itself much about it. I cannot think it is right and Christian, by means of pains and penalties, to force men to abstain from inoffensive and innocent work, or from inoffensive and innocent sport, even on Sunday. By *innocent*, I mean *that which is not wrong in itself*; and by *inoffensive*, I mean *that which does not disturb other men*. It might be right for the Legislature to pass a decree, that certain kinds of work should not be done on Sunday, if they would annoy the greater part of the people of the Commonwealth. If such a law is made, I should hope it might be made in the same spirit in which the laws command travellers to keep to the right; and not by any means to tyrannize over men's consciences. One thing, it seems to me, the Legislature has entirely in its power. Here are many Manufacturing Companies, having in their employment large numbers of men and women. The Legislature has created these Companies. It may, therefore, make laws, telling them when to shut down their gates, and stop their mills,—thus forbidding them to tyrannize over mankind, by forcing operatives to work on Sunday against their wishes, if such a disposition should ever exist. It may be necessary to do that, or unnecessary.

It is sometimes said that the present prevalent notions respecting Sunday, notwithstanding they are untrue, superstitious, and unchristian, are yet " safe," and therefore it is very improper to come forward and oppose them. Therefore this Convention is likely to be a very *wicked* Convention, although it should say nothing but what is true. I heard a man say, that if he had the whole of God Almighty's truth shut up in his left hand, he would not allow a man to unlock even his little finger. That is not my creed at all. I do not believe mankind is in the least danger of being ruined by an *excess of truth*. I have that confidence in truth, that I fear it not under any circumstances; but I do fear error, whether coming from churches, states, or majorities, or minorities, in the world.

This untrue doctrine has, already, not only deprived us of a great many advantages which we might receive on Sunday, but has brought numerous positive and dreadful evils upon us. In the first place, it has prevented the proper use of the Sunday. It has taught us to observe the Sunday, not for itself, but as a duty; to keep it from *fear*, and not from *love*. It has made it a day, stern, dark, and disagreeable, to at least one half of the people of this land.

Out of this notion, in the next place, there has grown this idea, that while, for common offences, God allows the natural laws of the universe to keep the even tenor of their way; while he sends no lightning to fall upon the man who steals, or who commits murder or the foulest crimes, yet for the purpose of punishing those who break the Sabbath, He works miracles; He overturns boats on the waters, strikes barns with lightning, and throws men from the tops of their hay-ricks; and thus overturns the laws of nature for the purpose of punishing the man who does what he might have done with a good conscience on Saturday or Monday. That notion has been sedulously promoted among the people. I know not the men engaged in this work. Some of them, I doubt not, are good men, and honest men. It is not for me to sit in judgment upon them. I will suppose they have walked by their light. I will not judge the men, but I will judge of their light by the manner of their walking.

Again, this popular notion about the Sunday works badly, by preventing reform meetings. It was my lot to pass ten years of my life in a little village not ten miles from Boston, where there was an Orthodox meeting. I think that minister sincere, as I am sincere; but no Temperance meeting, Peace meeting, or Anti-Slavery meeting, could be held in his church; not a marriage or a funeral could take place on Sunday. He could not hinder men from dying on that day, but he would hinder them from being buried. Now, all reforms find this a great obstacle in their way. Sunday is a leisure day. It is a day when it is thought wicked to read any secular book. It may be the best book that ever was written, but it is wrong to read it on Sunday. But the people don't think it is wicked to meet together in a church, and hear what is told them there. Sunday, therefore, would afford the very best opportunity for the reformer to do his work. On other days, the Temperance men, and the Anti-Slavery men, and the Peace men, find their hearers at work. The men who would substitute for the present modes of education, a wiser, and better, and bigger education of the people, cannot find an audience. The Sunday, then, would afford these Reformers a good opportunity of gaining access to men's hearts; but they are met at the very threshold of the church with, " It is the Lord's day; you must only preach the gospel." It is thought because it is Sunday, that the gospel on that day means nothing but what is purely theological. One may preach upon the damnation of infants, or ninety-nine hundredths of the whole human race, and not entrench upon the rules which fortify the Sunday. But if he shows that Intemperance is a crime; it is wrong to make rum, and to sell rum; it poisons people; it is wrong to fight the infamous war off there in Mexico, and to fight the battles on Sunday, — that moment he is thrust out of the church door, and told that the church is not the place for him, and Sunday is not the day for that. The same thing takes place in our day as in Christ's day. The child of the drunkard, and the orphan of the soldier butchered in Mexico, — these come to the reformer, and say, " Save us, cleanse us, help us ! " and the worshippers of the Sabbath say, as the Pharisees of old said, though I hope with better motives, " Are there not six days in which ye can come and be healed? Why not come then ? " This grows unavoidably out of this false doctrine, which we are told it is " safe " to let remain.

That is not all. The tendency is to make religion merely ceremonial. Some of the resolutions speak of it as such. I think a great deal of the ceremoniousness and sanctimoniousness of our religion has come from this idea; and, accordingly, we have seen this phenomenon presented constantly in a thousand shapes before us, of men so exceedingly scrupulous about the first day of the week, and so exceedingly unscrupulous on every other day. The moment we abolish *the superstition* connected with this, the moment we view the Sunday as Paul viewed it, and as all the Gentile Christians viewed it, as a day like other days, which it is expedient to devote to religious purposes, then all this host of evils stops at once, for the superstition I have mentioned is the mother of all these abominations.

It is no part of my plan " to give up the Sunday," to devote the day to business, to mere idleness, to mere amusement. I should be sorry to see it thus spent. We shall always have *work* enough in New England; and if Moses were to legislate for us, I think he would sooner have two rest-days in the week than abandon one. I would turn the Sunday into a day of rest for the body—a day devoted to rest—to religious, moral and intellectual culture, to social intercourse,—a day of freedom, not of bondage; still less a day of riot and license. I would shun the superstitions which now rob us of half the blessings of the Sunday, — but would not, as our Puritan fathers, go from one wrong to another wrong. I would not keep the Sunday like a fanatic ; I would not, like a fanatic, destroy it.

I promised not to speak long. I have spoken longer than I intended, and so I will say no more. I have a series of Resolutions which I will read and lay on the table. They differ somewhat from those of my friend, which have been already laid before you.

Resolved, 1st, That it is not our design to " give up the Sunday "—to prevent or diminish the voluntary devotion of that day to rest, and to special efforts for the spiritual culture of man ; but, on the contrary, it is our deliberate purpose yet farther to promote such an observance of the day, but without resorting to superstition or the force of public law to insure it.

2d. That though we regard all days as equally holy in themselves, and recognize the duty of keeping every day blameless and holy, by living a manly and religious life, we yet learn from history and from observation, that the custom of devoting one day in the week mainly to rest from common work, and to the various purposes of spiritual culture, has produced many happy results, and that it is still important to the greater part of mankind.

3d. That we desire to remove all obstacles which now hinder men from making the most profitable and Christian use of the Sunday.

4th. That we consider the common opinions concerning the origin of the Sabbath, and of the Sabbatical observance of Sunday, as also respecting the nature of that day itself, as untrue, as superstitious, hostile to the Christian spirit, and full of danger to the religious interests of mankind; that these unchristian and superstitious opinions form one of the chief obstacles to the yet more profitable use of the Sunday.

5th. That while we lament the prevalence of such opinions, and consider them as dangerous, we should also lament at seeing the Sunday devoted to common work or amusements—not as if we shared the common and erroneous opinions concerning the Sunday—not as if we thought it wicked to labor or sport on that day—but because we think it may be devoted to a higher and a better purpose.

6th. That we lament the attempts made and making to render the Sunday more Jewish in its character, thus attempting to lay a yoke on us which neither we nor our fathers were able to bear.

7th. That we consider Sunday a fit and proper time as any other day of the week to meet and discuss the sins of the people, such as War, Slavery, Intemperance, and the like—and also to take measures to prevent and exterminate these evils.

8th. That while we admit the Legislature has the right to make laws concerning the operations of manufacturing and other corporations which it has called into existence, on Sundays as on other days—and also to insure justice between the employer and employed—we deny that it has any moral right to legislate for the conscience of private men, by telling them when they shall worship God.

9th. That we recommend the repeal of all laws which decree penalties against private persons for the pursuit of innocent and inoffensive callings on the Sunday.

Mr. Garrison rose to make a few remarks on the ninth resolution of the series he had submitted to the Convention, relating to the awful judgments alleged to be consequent upon Sabbath-breaking.

The Rev. Dr. Edwards, (he proceeded,) in his " Permanent Sabbath Documents," has recorded various instances of " divine displeasure," exhibited toward those who were guilty of this most heinous sin, as terrible warnings to all persons to " remember the Sabbath day, and keep it holy."   But I hold in my hand the fragments of a most extraordinary work, written probably a century and a half ago, exclusively in elucidation and defence of the Sabbath—the name of its author unknown, but he appears to have been a minister in the city of London—occupying I know not how many pages, for the first 288 pages are missing, and at page 766 a large portion is evidently wanting—in which I find chronicled far more wonderful and miraculous interpositions of an incensed God, to punish the daring Sabbath-breaker,, than any recited in the Documents of the American and Foreign Sabbath Union; and I would suggest to Dr. Edwards the expediency of substituting these cases for his own, as still better adapted to make a " solemn " impression on the minds of the rising generation.   This voluminous work is entitled, " THE PRACTICAL SABBATARIAN," and is remarkable for its erudition, its antiquarian research, its quaintness of style, its power of amplification, its vehemence and severity of spirit, and its unsurpassed superstition and folly.   I will turn to Chap. XLIX. which treats of " God's Tremendous Judgments executed upon those who have prophaned and violated his holy Day," and which begins in the following appalling style:— " We have already seen, by Scripture light, frowns in the face of God, wrath in the heart of God, flaming in the eye of God, and a sword in the hand of God, against those who dare pollute his holy Sabbath."   As a specimen of the work, I will read a few passages from this chapter.

[Mr. Garrison proceeded to read a number of instances in which " God's Tremendous Judgments " were executed for the sin alleged.   A portion of these must suffice for this pamphlet.]

"One who carried corn into his barn upon the Lord's day, had it all consumed with fire from heaven, together with his house." It was, says the author, "the fire of God's wrath."

"One serving a writ of subpœna upon another, coming from church on the Lord's day, after some words of reproof for so doing, and a light answer thereunto, the person who served the writ died in the place, without speaking any more words. O the fearful and just judgment of the Lord! This profane person himself was subpœnaed unexpectedly by a writ he could not refuse, to appear before God's dreadful tribunal."

"A grazier's servant would needs drive his cattle on the Lord's day in the morning from the inn where he lay on the Saturday night; but he had not gone a stone's cast from the town, but he fell down dead suddenly, when he was in perfect health before. Thus the Lord's day is written in dominical letters, in the blood of transgressors who profane it."

"Sometimes God doth not presently cut off those who profane his day, but he puts a brand of infamy upon them, to make them a shame, and a terror to themselves, that they may be hissed off from the stage of the world, and with self-confounding and horror may go down unexpectedly to their graves. This is verified by this story:—There was an husbandman, who went to plough on the Lord's day, and cleansing his plough with an iron, the iron stuck so fast in his hand for two years, that he carried it about with him as a signal testimony of the Lord's just displeasure against him; and so he lived infamously in the world till he died, and made his passage to another world; the iron in his hand only discovering the adamant in his heart."

"In Helvetia, near Belessina, three men were playing at dice on the Lord's day, and in their play, one called Utricke Schrætorus, having hopes of a good cast, having lost much money before, he now expected fortune, or rather the devil, to succor him, and therefore he breaks out into this horrid blasphemy:— *If fortune deceive me now, I will thrust my dagger into the body of God, as far as I can.*   And so with a powerful force he throws it up towards heaven, which dagger was never seen more, and immediately five drops of blood fall before them all upon the table, and as suddenly came the devil among them, and carries away this vile wretch, with such a terrible and hideous noise, as the whole city was astonished at it. Those who remained endeavored to wipe off the blood, but to little purpose; for the more they rubbed, the more perspicuous and visible the blood was. Report carries it over the city; multitudes flock to see this wonder, who find those who have thus profaned the Sab] bath, rubbing the blood to get it out. These two men, who were the companions to him who was carried away by the devil, were by the decree of the Senate bound in chains, and as they were leading to prison, one of them was suddenly struck dead, and from his whole body a wonderful number of worms and vermin was seen to crawl. The city thus terrified with God's judgments, and to the intent that God might be glorified, and a future vengeance averted from the place, they caused the third offender, one of the gaming companions, to be forthwith put to death; and they caused the table, with the drops of blood upon it, to be preserved as a monument of God's wrath against this sin. Thus this blasted table, like Lot's wife, was a standing warning-piece, to cause all to take heed of Sabbath-breaking and ingratitude."

"A vintner who was a great swearer and drunkard, as he was standing at his door upon the Lord's day with a pot of wine in his hand to invite his guests, was by the wonderful justice and power of God carried into the air with a whirlwind, and never seen or heard of more. How soon can the word of God make the creature, and how suddenly can the wind of God destroy the sinner! Let us read and tremble."

"A great man using every Lord's day to hunt in sermon time, had a child by his wife, with a head like a dog, and it cried like a hound; and it had ears and chaps like the forementioned beast. This monstrous sin is most justly punished with a monstrous birth."

"Stratford upon Avon was twice on fire, and both times on the Lord's day, whereby it was almost consumed, and chiefly

5*

for profaning that blessed day, and contemning the word of God out of the mouth of his faithful ministers. And is it not just, that market towns should be laid waste, where the soul's market day is despised and profaned? And it is no wonder, if we make God's day the stage of sin, if he make our houses the fuel of his wrath."

"Whatever hand was used in London's fire, [1666,] it was Sabbath guilt which threw the first fire-ball to turn it into flames. When Mount Sinai was on fire and smoking, God was there, and that was the cause of the combustion; but when dear London was on fire, guilt was there, nay, Sabbath guilt, and this was the cause of its devastation and ruin. * * O tremendous judgment! Prayers could not divert the fire, nor tears quench it: the flames were above our attempts, and the Lord was against our entreaties; he was now truly angry with our prayers. No intercession can screen London from the consuming flames; but divine vengeance rides triumphantly in the midst of its spoils and victories. * * Who caused the fire to burn against as well as with the wind? Nay, who determined the place where the fire began, in the midst of pitch, tar, oil, hemp, powder, and all provocations of flames and ruin? Let us then take it for granted, some perfidious engineer of Rome hatched the plot; yet it could never have been fledged, had not God's indignation given wing to it. * * Whatever miscreant made the ball, God threw the fire, and turned this famous but sinful city into ashes. To accent his wrath, he did it upon his own blessed day. And will you know the reason? We made light of his Sabbath by our vanity, looseness and profaneness, and God hath set a mark upon it by firing, on this day, one of the best cities in the world."

If there be any legends of the Romish Church—if there be any fables in heathen mythology—more absurd, revolting, or impious than this catalogue of "God's tremendous judgments," I have yet to peruse them. Yet fabrications like these are circulated far and wide, even at the present day, especially by the American and Foreign Sabbath Union, in the documents prepared by their General Agent, the Rev. Justin Edwards, D. D. Is it possible that such men can be honest or sincere? Do they not know that they are guilty of vile imposture? Many terrific stories do they tell about the inflictions of an angry God upon Sabbath-breakers; but how does it happen that we never hear of the idolatrous, the covetous, the adulterous, being visited in this manner? Is the fourth commandment the only one in the Decalogue, the violation of which excites the special displeasure of Heaven? Is not the first commandment as dear to God as the fourth, allowing the latter to be as holy and as binding as you please? But if a person should manufacture or worship any number of idols here, would any one expect to see him struck dead, or his house consumed by fire, on that account? If he should violate the sixth commandment, would he thereby subject himself to the liability of being killed by a flash of lightning, or swallowed by an earthquake? If not, why not? Will Sabbatarians answer the question? But, no! God is not moved to interpose miraculously to blast any other transgressor than the Sabbath-breaker! A strict observance of the Sabbath is the object of his highest solicitude; and to secure that, he is ready at any moment to smite with his thunderbolts the man who esteems every day alike! And why is this? O, because it is *the day of the priesthood;* the day on which they get their gain, and assert their authority; the day on which they hold absolute mastery over the people, and claim to be listened to as God-sent; the day for promoting and perpetuating their craft! Why should they not bring in God to smite us, who will not hallow their harvest day, nor recognize as valid their spurious credentials? Do you not see why it is that they attempt to frighten the unreflecting in this manner? Clearly, it must be apparent to all who have any vision.

The resolutions were further discussed by A. Bronson Alcott and George W. Haskell.

Adjourned to meet at seven o'clock.

Evening Session.

Met pursuant to adjournment, the President in the chair. The various resolutions before the Convention having been read, C. C. Burleigh said—

This morning, in supporting a resolution which denounces legislation in regard to Sabbath observances, as despotic and unconstitutional, I endeavored to show that, even if we admit the correctness of the views of the first day Sabbatarians,—if we suppose that the law for the observance of a whole day is permanent and universal, and that it has but undergone a change as to the particular day to be observed, but not as to the observance of a day,—still, the Legislature has no right to compel men to do this religious duty. It has no more right to compel them to observe the Sabbath, than to compel them to attend the religious assembly, or listen to the preaching; no more than to compel them, if you please, to entertain strangers, for which we have an express apostolic command. If I mistake not, we are told to be mindful to entertain strangers; for, in so doing, some have even entertained angels unawares. But who would thence infer, that the Legislature has the right to turn every man's house into a tavern, and compel him to throw open his doors to all who may choose to enter? It may be his duty to be hospitable, but it is one of those duties which the Legislature cannot enforce. If, then, the Legislature cannot enforce what is universally admitted to be a duty, what even those who refuse to do it will not deny to be a duty, how can it have a right to enforce the observance of that as a duty, which a large proportion of the people do not consider as such, which they protest against, and the doing of which they consider, in many cases, will be rather injurious than beneficial?

This evening, I propose to look at the subject from another point of view. Thus far, the argument which I have presented proceeds upon the admission, that the Sabbath worshippers may be right in their doctrine, and only wrong in trying to force it upon other people. But I deny, and in my remarks this evening shall endeavor to show that I have good reason for denying, that the doctrine which they thus try to force upon me, and upon you, is a true doctrine, trying it by the standard to which themselves appeal, the Scriptures of the Old and New Testaments. I deny that they have any Scripture authority for setting apart one day of the week as peculiarly holy, and requiring, I will not say by legislative enactments, but even by theological appeal, by holding up the fear of the punishment of the transgression of God's law, the observance of that day as holy time. They err doubly; they violate the Constitution of the country, and the principle of the freedom of conscience; and they do it to enforce the reception of error, the conformity of the subjects of their legislation to heresy in doctrine. Where is the warrant? The burden of proof certainly lies upon those who affirm the existence of such an institution; and where is the warrant for the requirement of the observance of the first day of the week as a Sabbath? Where is the Scripture proof, that God has commanded the people of this age, and of this country,—the people of any age, except that of Moses, and of the Jewish commonwealth or theocracy,—of any people, except the Israelitish nation,—where is the evidence that he has required, in any other age and of any other people, the observance of a holy day?

The advocates of the first day Sabbath, I know, are ready with their Scripture quotations. I never met with one, but almost in the next breath, after the positive assertion of the doctrine, he would give m the Fourth Commandment; and if I was not satisfied with that, would give me a quotation or two from some other part of the Old Testament. But do these quotations authorize the inference drawn from them? The Fourth Commandment I may suppose the main pillar of the whole fabric of argumentation for the alleged Scripture authority:—"Remember the Sabbath day, to keep it holy; for in six days," &c. This, then, is the warrant for keeping the first day of the week in a manner widely different from that in which the Jews were required to keep the seventh day of the week! I object to this kind of reasoning, in the first place, because it does not touch my case at all, nor your case at all. A com-

mandment given to the Jewish nation is no law for us. We
are under no obligation to obey it. Unless you can give me
some other reason for observing the first day of the week, or
any day of the week, as holy, you must either give up the argument, or carry the Jewish code right through, with all its stringent provisions. What right have you to take one ceremony,
and leave another? What right have you to take a Sabbath,
and yet not the Sabbath of the Hebrew law giver? What right
have you to reject the penalty for the violation of the Sabbath,
—of being stoned to death? What right have you to take this
observance, and not take the ceremonial purifications enjoined
in the Jewish law? Why neglect strict conformity to its
requirements, even in the manner of observing the Sabbath,
which the Jews acknowledged to be binding upon them? The
day set apart for the Jewish nation, and for that alone, is no
day for us. We are under no requirement on that ground to
observe it.

But men say, The Sabbath institution is in the moral law;
it is not in the ceremonial law. Why, it is among the Ten Commandments; and don't you know that the Westminster Catechism says, that the Ten Commandments comprehend the
moral law? There is Scripture to prove all that is needful.
There is the testimony of the Westminister divines, an authority but little below that of the Scriptures themselves, — that the
moral law is summarily comprehended in the Ten Commandments; meaning that each of the Ten Commandments constitutes a portion of the moral law, and all of them constitute the
essence of the whole moral law. We are told, You admit that
we ought not to worship idols? Yes. And ought not to profane that which is sacred? Yes. And ought to honor our
parents? Yes. And ought not to steal, or kill, or commit
adultery, or lie, or covet the goods of our neighbors? All very
true. Then why ought we not to observe the first day of the
week as the Sabbath, when that commandment is in the same
list of ordinances with all the others, which you admit to be
binding? Because I do not admit these to be binding; *i. e.*
I do not admit that my obligation to obey them is derived from

the decalogue. I do not admit that, because these commandments were given to the Jews, they were therefore given to
me. I believe I must obey them, not because they were given
to the Jews, but because their own nature is right; and when
you can show me anything else which is right, any other duty
growing out my nature and my relations to other beings,
then I will admit that I must do that also. Can you prove this
with regard to the Sabbath institutions? The Sabbatarians go
to the letter, and not to the spirit; and the very fact that
they rest their argument upon the command of the decalogue
is, to say the least, a very strong presumptive evidence, that
they have no other ground upon which to base it. They do
not base their argument against murder upon the sixth Commandment; nor do they rest upon the first, to show that we
ought to worship the only true God; but they go to the principles of essential morality — they go to the instinct of reverence — they go to the nature of man, and of man's relations to
man, and to his Maker. You go there for your proof of the
wrongfulness of killing and of idolatry, and of the duty to worship the proper object of religious veneration. Why don't
you go there, then, to make out a case for Sabbath observance?

But we are told that the institution does not begin with the
Fourth Commandment. That was only a sort of declaratory
setting forth of the existence of a law previously enacted.
When God created the world in six days, and thereafter rested
from all the work which he had created and made, he sanctified that day of rest, and enjoined it upon all men, that in
memory of the completion of the work of creation, they should
rest also, and rest just as long as he rested. We are told, in
almost the beginning of the Bible, that God created the world
in six days, and rested on the seventh day; and he therefore
blessed the seventh day, and hallowed it. Suppose this to be
all a *literal* truth; does it follow, because He hallowed
it, that you and I are bound to hallow it also? Does the
account say *how* God hallowed it — for what end or purpose
he blessed it? Does it say that he blessed it as a day for me

to devote entirely to religious worship, to the study of religious truth, and to what I may call technical theology? Is not the very lameness of the argument a very strong evidence against you? Men do not lean upon a broken staff, when they have a strong and whole one upon which they can lean. They do not trust to a feeble defence, when they have an impregnable fortress, behind which they can retire. Where is the proof that God requires men to do anything? I see no more proof that God required men to rest, from the statement that He rested, than I see proof that He required men to create a world, from the statement that He created one. We might as well say, that it is our duty to get up every Monday morning, and go to creating light, and earth, and sun, and stars, and trees, and animals, and men, as to say that we are bound on the seventh day to rest, because God rested on that day, and on account of his rest hallowed that day. You have no proof that such is our duty; it is only your inference.

But I object again to this kind of reasoning — for we not only have no proof in favor of the literal construction of the history of the creation, but have further very clear and strong proof against that literal construction. If I am to take the testimony interpreted in the lights of modern science, or, in other words, if I am to make the history agree with modern discoveries and undeniable facts, we should have a much longer day of rest than I understand the most zealous Sabbatarian to ask for. Geologists have discovered in the bosom of the earth, evidence that the process of creation, from the first existence of chaotic matter to the final arrangement of all these harmonious relations of thing to thing, of being to being, occupied not days or periods of twenty-four hours each; not six periods equal to the revolutions of the earth about its axis in these days, but six periods, or whatever number of periods you choose to divide it into, of a length that, tried by any standard of our comprehension, might be called infinite. Certainly our imagination can give no bounds to them. Ages piled upon ages must have passed between the existence of the first chaotic mass, and the presence of that beauty, and harmony, and animation, which we now behold. You may say, " This is not in the Bible." It was said to me, the other day, " Such and such learned men might have said it, but it is not in the Bible." Suppose that it is not in the Bible which Moses wrote, in the records which flowed from the pens of men; nevertheless, it is in a Bible, a Bible as unerring, and whose revelations are as true as any other Bible or revelations to which you can possibly appeal. It is the declaration of the Creator himself — the revelation of God's will made manifest in God's act — the testimony of the Divine Mind, lithographed in the eternal rocks; and until these rocks shall moulder away, until this earth shall melt, and its elements dissolve with fervent heat, that record stands there, to contradict all your ephemeral theories which are based upon demonstrated falsehood.

Now, if you admit the soundness of the deductions of geological science, — if you admit what the most pious souls and most learned men do now admit,—what every intelligent theologian, who compares theology with general science, will admit, — what your Andover, your Princeton, your New Haven, your Newton, and your Hamilton Professors will admit, — what the more intelligent of all the clergy in the land will admit, — that these periods of earth's creation were periods of years, of ages inconceivably long in duration, then we have hardly got to the day-dawn of the first Sabbath yet. Six periods have rolled away in the process of creation, and the seventh being equal to each of them, that is being one-sixth part as long as the transition from chaos to harmony, it must reach on, I know not how many ages into the future. The Mosaic time of the completion of the creation is only about six thousand years ago; and that would be but a few minutes marked out upon the dial-plate of the great clock of the universe, where suns, whose cycles require millions of millions of years for their accomplishment, are but the minute-hands moving slowly along to indicate the time. Your Sabbath will be a long time finishing; and we ought to adopt, on other ground than that mentioned this morning, a system of legislation which shall forbid all work.

Oh, no; only one-seventh part of the time is to be observed as sacred. Very well, then; but why do you require me to measure my time with your yardstick? If I agree to your supposition, that the ordinance is, to have six periods for work, and then another period for rest, no matter of what length, since we must have different periods from those originally employed by the Creator. Or perhaps, we should have periods bearing about the same length in proportion to His, that our nature, or our quantity of being, if I may be allowed the expression, bears to His; then what is that proportion? How do we know that one day of twenty-four hours is any nearer right than one week, or a month, or a year, or an hour, or five minutes? Where do you find the rule or standard of judgment? I say, perhaps, that I will take one-seventh of the time; but, instead of taking twenty-four hour periods, I prefer to take one-seventh, or about three hours and a half, out of every twenty-four hours. How will that do? I cannot take the very same length which the Creator took; is there any rule but that of expediency, to which you can appeal for the settlement of this difficulty? If you say, "We take one day, because it is more convenient; a longer period would make the rest-season burdensome and monotonous, and in fact worse than toil, and a shorter would not be enough for rest; one would be too wide, and the other too narrow, an interval;" then you come right upon the ground of expediency at once; and it is for you to demonstrate that it is better to work six days, and rest the seventh, than to take a longer or shorter period of time. It is for you to demonstrate that more will be accomplished, less endured, that man's physical, moral, and mental nature, will grow more vigorously, more symmetrically, under the influence of this division of time, than under any other division; and where is the proof of that? Where can you find the evidence which will satisfy the inquiring mind upon a point of that character? I think you have not found it yet. The very fact, that the Sabbatarians appeal to the literal record is an evidence that they have not found it; for if they had, they would not need to float ever upon those texts of doubtful interpretation, to make the best of them.

Again, the theory upon which this whole system is based, lacks the evidence of its authority in another point; not only in failing to present correctly the picture of the process of the world's creation, but also in giving us a false view of the character and action of the world's Creator. We are taught to believe that God rested from his work, in the sense of absolute cessation, just as if God could rest; in other words, just as if the central essence of all action, the motive-power of all motion, could ever be still. Can you conceive of a motive-power that is not moving? a primal cause not causing? a cause producing no effect? I think that Jesus spoke the language of a deep and true philosophy, although he spoke against the theology of his times, when he said, "My Father worketh *hitherto*," *quite up to this point*, "and I work." Do you not see the evidence of his works all around you? Will the Sabbatarian deny that "in Him we live, and move, and have our being?" Are we living, and moving, and having our being, in an inert substance, that which is not active, but resting from all the work which He has made? If He is the essence and author of our life, the vitality whereby we exist, then what becomes of the argument, based upon the assumption that this vital power of the universe, the source of its respiration, ceases to be a breathing being? They who argue in favor of Sabbath worship admit that not a sparrow falls to the ground without his notice, and that all the powers of nature are but the modes of divine action. This power, which is wheeling the heavenly bodies in their orbits — this power, which is calling the vegetation from the soil, which is clothing the earth with beauty, or in genial showers refreshing the thirsty land,—which is pouring upon us the beautiful sun-light with its flow of active enjoyment; all these processes of nature are but the modes of divine action. Did the plants he had created stop growing on the first Sabbath? Did the streams stop flowing? Did the sun cease shining? Did the stars cease to give forth their rays? Did the music of the morning stars, when they sang together of the glory of God, and all the sons of God shouted for joy, fall to a dead silence until the day of rest was over-past? "My Father worketh hitherto;" He writes out the record of His doings continually; He is continually tracing new scriptures upon all the works he has unrolled to the gaze of man; and thus He is ever writing the truth upon the innermost tablet of the human soul. This outward action is but the outward symbol, the exterior manifestation and indication of the still deeper and nobler, the still more intense action that is ever going on in the soul of man; and if you can lay your finger-point upon that moment of time, in which this divine activity ceases, and can lift your finger again before it crumbles back to dust, or to its original nothing, then we will listen to your argument, based upon God's seventh day of rest.

But, admitting the institution of the Sabbath, notwithstanding the difficulties in which we are involved, we must go to the letter of the record, and cling to that, and we find another difficulty in explaining the entire silence of the early records as to the actual observance of such a day. We are told of their sacrifices and prayers; of various religious observances and moral duties of life; of the exercise of hospitality; of neighborly deeds of kindness; of words of counsel between friend and friend; of the intimate domestic union in the families of the patriarchs; of the words of love which passed between Abraham and Lot, and Abraham and Sarah; of those who stood in the most confidential relations to each other; and in all these scriptures, where the private histories of the patriarchs are thus enrolled before our eyes, is it not marvellous, is it not a miracle almost, that not the simplest mention, or slightest intimation, is anywhere to be found in all these ancient histories, of an institution ordained of heaven, which in modern days is found to be the sun of the moral universe. I am not archæologist enough to solve all the riddles of antiquity, and this certainly puzzles me.

Passing over that, we come down to the clear proof of the appointment of the Sabbatical institution. Under what circumstances, and for what purpose, was it formed? We are told expressly, that it was established as a peculiar symbol to designate a peculiar tribe of men. It was given to the Jew, in contradistinction to all then existing nations, and not only that, but to the generation then being, in contradistinction to all preceding generations. Not to your fathers, but "to you, who are here alive this day." It would seem as if the phraseology was fashioned with direct reference to the possible arising of the question, at some future day, as to when the Sabbath was instituted; and as if there might be an attempt to carry its origin farther back than the exodus from Egypt. "All you who are here alive *this day*." For *you*, and not for the whole race of Abraham, or the stock of Shem, or the descendants of Adam; for you who are *here*, and here *alive*, and not your fathers; and lest some broader acceptation should be put upon it, it is for you who are here alive *this day*. Now a man who, out of a book containing this testimony, could elaborate such a splendid superstructure of argument as to sustain the modern Sabbath, must indeed have some such power as that which created the world *out of nothing* in six days.

So far, then, we find no Sabbatical institution, excepting one peculiar to the Jew. I object further, then, to the argument of the Sabbatarian, that, even if the command is binding upon us now, we do not keep it. They do not keep it, who insist upon its being a binding command. I have already intimated that they have changed the day. Besides that, they do not keep it in the mode prescribed. The Jew could not bear any burden on that day. The Jew could not go out of the camp, or go a mile in any direction, a much shorter distance than many a minister rides to meeting. He gets into a carriage, driven by a hired driver, and goes much farther than the command allows him. The Jews were not allowed to prepare their food, or to kindle fires in their houses, on that day. I know not exactly how we are to interpret that in our climate, so as to keep the command in our winters, unless it be that anthracite coal was designed to help the matter by enabling us to build our fire on Saturday night, and to put in coal enough to last till Monday morning. But what are they to do, who have not these means

6*

of keeping a fire? The Jewish Sabbath was a rest-day. Your Sabbath is a day of activity of some kind or other. The very class of men who are most earnest in inculcating the most rigid observance of the day, do the principal part of their work, and earn the principal part of their living, on that day. I have no objection to their working on that day, nor to their receiving the means of subsistence for it, provided they will be consistent with themselves, and not send me to the county jail, because I am trying to do what I consider my duty on that day. We do not observe the Sabbath as a rest-day.

The primary object of the Jewish Sabbath was not religious assembling; that was secondary. We have turned it the other way. We make it a day of religious observance for the sake of religious observance, and then we enjoin upon ourselves a rest, with certain privations and qualifications of a very indefinite breadth. We except from restriction " works of necessity and mercy." What are works of necessity and mercy? If a man goes out into the field, and gathers a quantity of grain, that the hungry may be fed, he is not doing a work of necessity. But if he hires a woman to go into his kitchen, and take that same grain when ground, and sift the flour and bake it, that is a matter of necessity; the family must have something to eat. And what are works of mercy? May I plead the cause of the down-trodden slave in Southern lands? Oh no, you must wait until Monday evening. May I plead for the poor victim of intemperance? No, that is not a proper subject for holy time. May I demand by the power of argument, and appeals of truth, the regulation of all human action, so as not to stand in the way of the unfolding of man's whole being in the sunlight of God's truth and love? May I endeavor to modify the institutions of the country, so as to harmonize them with the laws of God, and with man's nature? Oh no, that would be lecturing on politics, or political economy, or secular business. And so on to the end of the chapter; these are not works of mercy.

I am, I suppose, justified in lifting an ox or a sheep out of a pit, because we find the letter of the text for that; and men do not like to go in the face of the letter, though sometimes they contrive to get behind it, and accomplish their purposes in spite of it. They leave a broad margin to the command, and one man will interpret it this way and another that way; and have we any limit? And if we have not, have not I as good a right to decide for myself as you have? Is the Legislature to decide for me, in accordance with your notions, any more than to decide for you in accordance with mine? Has the theologian any right to come in and tell me, "Thus far God permits you to go, but no farther"? I ask for his authority, and he cannot give the authority. It is not in the letter, it is not in the spirit. We have departed from the old Jewish Sabbath, both as to the day and the manner of its observance. How can we pretend to have built upon their foundation, when we have departed so far that the centre of gravity has almost ceased to be supported by it? No wonder that the Sabbatarians are alarmed at every breath of air, lest the superstructure which they have erected should come tumbling about their ears.

In reply to this it is said, that the Jewish system, as a Jewish system, is not binding upon us; it is only the moral law in the ten commandments, and that command has been so far changed as to allow, and even to require, our observing the first day of the week, instead of the seventh; for Christ rose upon the first day, and it is a divine decree that we should keep Sunday, and not Saturday. First, there is the assumption,—and it is assumption all the way,—that any part of the ten commandments is the moral law; next, that the law being divine, we have a right to change it in one particular, while we cling to it in another; and then the assumption, that it ever has been changed by anything more than mere human caprice. Does God change His own fixed permanent laws? Is His moral law one thing to-day, another yesterday, and another to-morrow? Was it, "Thou shalt not kill," ages ago; and is it now that we may kill Mexicans, or fight duels—or does it except the man who has been guilty of murder, or arson, or rape, or any one of the crimes for which the statute of the State dooms to death? Do you so understand the essential right, the inherent law of things? What is God's law but the transcript of Himself, and how can it change? If, therefore, the Sabbatical law was ever a moral law, it is still a moral law, and can no more be changed than the nature of Him who made it.

Overlooking that difficulty, we meet a difficulty in the letter at the next step. Paul tells us, and he is considered pretty good authority, that this law, written on tables of stone, was THE MINISTRATION OF DEATH, and that it is done away; and he identifies the ten commandments by these two marks. It was the law " graven upon stones," and we have no evidence that any other part of the law was graven upon stone; and it was the law, upon the bringing of which from the mountain, the face of Moses shone so that he was obliged to cover it, which is a circumstance coupled with the delivery of no other part of the Mosaic code. Paul was pointing directly at the ten commandments, when he called that law a ministration of death, and spoke of it as done away. Of course, no man, who has brain enough to put two ideas together within its compass without their quarrelling there, will thence infer that the obligation to do right is done away. No man would say that, because the rude mountain hut is swept away by the tornado, therefore the granite on which it was based is crumbling to dust. The law of Moses commanded certain right things. It was as wrong to kill before the law of Moses as after, and therefore you are thrown back upon the original obligation. It was as wrong to steal, or to lie, or to covet, before the law of Moses as after, and therefore you are obliged to fall back to the original prohibition, which Moses did not create, and could not create, and which no abolition of the Mosaic code could affect. It is right for us to do certain things, and to leave others undone, not because there is written upon stone, or wood, or wax, or parchment, or paper, a declaration to that effect, but because such is the law of our being, such is the instinct of our nature, such is the decree of God to our own souls that we cannot deny, that we cannot escape from,—which makes the Gentiles without a written law, and yet doing things according to law, to be a law unto themselves. That inward law, without which, your written statute is good for nothing at all, still governs us.

"But if you throw away a part of the Bible, you may throw it all away." And how are we to know which is the moral law? Must we not judge for ourselves? Does Moses write heads over his different chapters,—Chap. I. and Chap. II. of the Ceremonial Law, and Chap. I. and Chap. II. of the Moral Law? If Moses had written out each precept on separate slips of paper, and then put them in his turban, and mixed them all together, they could not have been more completely blended and confused than they now are. You cannot tell, by any indications in the book, which is the ceremonial, and which is the moral; and how can you tell? By reading the book under the light of the candle of the Lord, which shineth into your heart. You are obliged, in reading, to determine which is the moral law, by the very same light by which I ask you to determine the question of right and wrong. To pick out the moral statutes from the text, you are first to determine what is a moral statute; and so you use your record as a good woman used her snuffers. They were mighty convenient, she said, when she snuffed the candle with her fingers, and then put the snuff into the snuffers! The work which is to be done by the help of the moral law in the record, you must do first, in order to get hold of the moral law there to do it with.

Again, we find this difficulty in the way of the assertion, that the fourth commandment of the decalogue is a part of the moral law. We can appeal to the letter, the letter to which our opponents themselves appeal most confidently. We ask, what was the testimony of Jesus upon that subject? He says, concerning your Sabbatical institution, that it is purely ceremonial; and this is the way he says it. When his disciples had violated that institution,—when they had gone through the field, and gathered a small quantity of wheat, and threshed it out, (for it was threshing on a small scale, and involved the same principle as if they had threshed out a dozen sheaves,)—when they had thus reaped, and gathered in, and threshed the grain, and then taken it to mill, and ground and *bolted* it, the Pharisees, applying to that the Mosaic law, said, "You have done wrong! Master, teach these fellows of yours better morality than this!" And he replies, in substance, "They do not need any better morality than this." He justified the act of his disciples, and justified it, too, by appealing to facts in their own history. Have you not read of the priests in the temple, who profane the Sabbath, and are blameless? Could he have said that the priests of the temple commit murder, and are blameless? that they bear false witness, and are blameless? Could he have said, with regard to anything contrary to essential right, They are rebels against God, and violaters of the rights of man, and are yet blameless? No; nothing which is a moral duty can be left undone, no moral principle can be violated, and yet he who violates the law be blameless. But he says, My disciples are just as blameless as your priests.

Again he says, "Have ye not read what David did when he was an hungered? How he went into the house of God, and did eat the shew-bread, which was not lawful for him to eat, but only for the priests? In other words, this is what he said — Your Sabbatical institution stands side by side with the institution of the shew-bread, and there is no more moral obligation in it. If that is not the meaning of his argument, it is illogical; and I do not know that those who claim the Sabbath as a moral institution will venture such an assertion upon the reasoning of Jesus. He classes this with mere ritual observances, among the things which were but a shadow of things to come. Then, of course, there is no moral obligation in it; it is a question of pure expediency, whether we shall observe it or not. Therefore, says he, the Son of Man is lord even of the Sabbath day. In what sense? In any other than this that he could set it aside? Could Jesus set aside a moral law of God? Could Jesus annul any one of the principles of divine government? Will any man say it? No, no. Then Jesus could not have been lord of the Sabbath day, unless the Sabbath was a merely ceremonial institution. If it was a moral institution, he could not have said it.

But there comes a reason which he claims, and which the Sabbatical champions are very fond of quoting. It was quoted, the other day, as a solemn warning for me to prevent my coming to this Convention — "It cannot be as you say; for Jesus expressly declares, that the Sabbath was made for man." This way of using scripture is just about upon a par with that of a pious Christian, who was offended by the vanity of his congregation, with their splendid knots, and ribbons, and gay flowers, and took for his text from which to preach against them, "Top-knot, come down!" It was in the Bible, and he gave the chapter and verse. When they returned home, they naturally enough looked it out, and found it to read, "Let him that is upon the house-*top not come down* to take anything out of his house." So here we have a passage taken right out of its connection, and absolutely turned from its true meaning. It is a worse perversion than that just alluded to; for there the sentence was simply taken, without reference to its previous meaning, and the meaning given to it was in nothing contradictory to it; but here is a contradiction in the use which is made of the text, to the meaning which Jesus evidently had when he spoke the words. The Sabbath was made for man; *for man*, not in contradistinction to for the *Jew*, but in contradistinction to *over* man, *controlling* man; it was made for man, and not man for the Sabbath. The Sabbath, he implied, is a mere institution, which, so long as it does man any good, is for his use.

I may say, garments are made for men, and not men for garments. Does it follow that a man is to wear his present garments forever? He may outgrow them, or he may shrink until, to use a homely expression, they shall hang about him like a meal-bag about a bean-pole. Must he still wear them, because the garments are made for man? When a man has outgrown his garment, or worn it out, he gets a new one; and he has just as good a right to throw away the institutions of another age which he has outgrown or worn out, as to throw away his garment. He may use the Sabbath to-day for one purpose, and to-morrow for another. To-day he may wear a

coat, and to-morrow make it a vest, or he may toss it over
to the good woman to turn it into carpet-rags. The institution is for man, and not man for the institution. It is a
Chinese custom to put wooden shoes on the feet of the
female children, and keep them there till they have grown
up to womanhood. Is there anything to compel us to put
on the wooden shoes of the men of the time of Moses,
and go clattering about with them upon the floors of
Christian churches, stumbling at every step? We want the
evidence, then, that the ceremonial observance of the Jew is
fitted to our wants at this day, before we can receive it as
binding upon us. Let the argument for it be based upon its
fitness. Let the holy day be for man, and not superior to
him — subordinate, and not controlling. As the image of one
of the heathen gods, in his ancient temple, is said to be so
large, and the roof so low, that if once he could be animated
and rise up, his head would burst the roof, and come out into
the clear atmosphere of heaven; so it is high time that some of
our sleeping deities should rise up, and see whether the temples are big enough to hold them. I do not believe that they
are. I do not believe that our institutions are large enough to
suit such men as we find now-a-days. I have no doubt that
there are dwarfs, who even now find them large enough, but
not those who have grown somewhat nearer to the stature of
perfect men; and it seems to me unreasonable to accommo-
date them to the dwarf who can creep about beneath their feet.

[A *voice*. Tell us more about the old clothes.]

"Old clothes" will suit the Jew, but we profess to have outgrown them. We have now the pattern of a higher type of
humanity, I had almost said, than Moses ever dreamed of.
We are taught to grow up to the stature of perfect men in
Christ Jesus. If Christ Jesus is a model so large that a perfect man can grow up in it, I ask if you can, in his name,
cramp that perfect man, or one even approaching perfection of
manhood, in the tattered garments that the Jew wore out long
ago? Can you put upon him that which neither they nor their
fathers were able to bear? I ask, then, how a man professing

to be a Christian, whose duty it is to grow up to manliness, can, I will not say require other men, but can submit himself to these ordinances of the past, and regard them as anything more than a mere means to an end, and even that answered by a better means now, and which ought therefore to be abolished?

You appeal still to the letter, and say that the early Christians changed the day from the seventh to the first. Go to the letter, and prove it. If you have it there, show me the text — show me the word, the syllable, the letter, I will not say which proves, but which goes to prove, that they changed it. The disciples met together, they say, on the first day of the week, in the evening, for religious worship. In the first place, it is sheer assumption that they met for religious worship. Perhaps it was for social intercourse. They might have met together to talk over the events which had just happened, to cheer each other's hearts, and to nerve each other up to take that manly stand which they afterwards did take. There is no proof that they spent it in a manner analagous in any way to religious worship. If meeting together to call in question the sanctity of time-honored institutions is keeping the day, then we keep Sunday when we talk against keeping it; then every lecture for reform, delivered upon that day, is a Sunday-keeping lecture of the best sort. That is, indeed, observing "the most venerable day of the Sun," the source of moral light.

You find no testimony in the record, that the disciples employed their time in what is now called religious worship; but suppose that they did, it is not proved that the day is peculiarly sacred for that reason. You hold a religious meeting, which you call a monthly concert of prayer for the conversion of the world. Suppose that some theologian of coming ages, who has contrived to keep his eyes bandaged, and shut out the light of the moral world and the theological science beaming upon him, so as still to hold to these Sabbatical institutions, should read in the history of this people, that they met for worship on the first Monday evening of every month, and

should say that, therefore, it is holy time; it is peculiarly
sacred; in it thou shalt not do any work. Would you not consider that absurd reasoning? Of course you would. Is it not
equally absurd, when it is said that Paul went into the syna-
gogue on the Jewish Sabbath, and met with the disciples on
the first day of the week, to infer that Paul kept either day as
holy, as a Jewish or a " Christian" Sabbath?

Again, one of the writers of the New Testament declares,
that he was in the spirit on the Lord's day. But does he say
what day it was? And if it was the first day of the week,
does this prove any peculiar sanctity in it? Do not men, on
other days, sometimes feel that they are in the spirit; that the
atmosphere all around them is radiant with cloven tongues of
fire, sitting upon each of them? Is not the Pentecost season
sometimes spread out over more than one day in seven? He
was in the spirit on the Lord's day. Would that prove that
everybody else was in the same spirit at the same time? or
that everybody else must observe that time in just the same
way, whether in the same spirit or not? And unless you know
both of these, you have no just reason for inferring that you
must do just as he did, even if you knew what that was. Certainly it is not a good argument for our doing a particular
thing, that he did it, unless you can make the conditions as
well as the circumstances the same. That is one objection we
have against the Sabbatical observances. They are building
up the ceremonial walls so high that the spirit has not room to
expand, or to catch the sunlight, and we are foregoing the
spirit of truth and goodness for the sake of the mere form of
it. We cling to the husk, after the ear has departed. We are
wearing the old garment still, when, instead of warming and
sheltering us, it is a tattered robe, which every breeze will
blow aside, and show our nakedness.

You have no proof in the Scriptures, then, that it was the apostles' custom to observe the first day of the week as a Sabbath.
But then profane history tells us about it. Profane history says
that the disciples used to meet before light, on the first day of the
week, and sing hymns to Christ as to a God. Suppose they did

meet, and go through these ceremonies; does this, any more than their meeting in the evening, as already spoken of, prove the holiness of the time? No more than our week-day meetings prove the same thing of the times on which they are held. Besides, here is another difficulty. The Bible is, of course, to be interpreted by the same rules of interpretation which apply to other ancient records — that is, according to the usages of the age and country in which it was written. Now you know that the people of that day, the people out of whom came the disciples, reckoned their time from evening till evening. If you are to take the observance of the evening of the first day of the week as a proof that the time was peculiarly holy, it would be an argument more for Monday than for Sunday; for Monday had begun on that evening. Or if you are to carry back the reckoning to prove the sanctity of Sunday, from their assembling on the evening of that day, why do you not take the meetings which began at or near midnight between Saturday and Sunday, and carry them back to prove the duty of observing the Jewish Sabbath? There is no doctrine claiming to be Christian, which is so destitute of Scripture authority as the doctrine of the first day Sabbath observance.

But our argument does not rest upon the entire absence of proof in favor of it. We have evidence that the apostles of Jesus, and that Jesus himself, did not observe times and days. Whatever Jesus did contrary to the Sabbatical law of the seventh day, goes against the observance of any day; for he had as yet given none in the place of it, and if any, then that was binding, and all his miracles upon that day are proofs that he did not regard it. The apostle, in effect, declares it is not a holy day. "One man esteemeth one day above another; another esteemeth every day alike; let every man be fully persuaded in his own mind." Would Paul say so about any principle of essential morality? Would he say, One man esteemeth it right to defraud, to lie, to wrong his neighbor, and another does not; one man esteemeth it right to love, another to hate; let every man be fully persuaded in his own mind? No; he would not use such language. Again he says, " Let no man judge you in meat or drink, or in respect of a holy day, or of the new moon, or of the Sabbath days, which are a shadow of things to come." And again he says to the Galatians, " Oh, foolish Galatians, ye observe days, and months, and times, and years ; I am afraid of you, lest I have bestowed upon you labor in vain." What proof is that, of his having labored with them in vain, if he had not labored to bring them out of that narrow dispensation, and to persuade them that they ought not to regard one day as peculiarly sacred — that they ought not to ascribe holiness to times and seasons ? It seems to me a perfectly clear case.

You say that Paul alluded to the Jewish ceremonial Sabbaths, and not the first day of the week, or the Sabbath of the decalogue; but what evidence have you ? He does not say so. He makes no exception in favor of *any* Sabbath. How, then, do you know that he meant to save any one from his general condemnation ? By tracing back, it is said, step by step, the Church history to that time. But where are the links of that chain of evidence which will prove to us that he kept the Sabbath, and that when he speaks about Sabbaths, and days, and times, and seasons, he did not mean those Sabbaths, but only Jewish festivals ? Besides, your attempted distinction runs against this difficulty ; he says, " an holy day," as well as " the Sabbath days," showing that he did not believe Christians were bound to keep *any* day as peculiarly holy.

Moreover, in an epistle supposed to be Paul's, he says, " There remaineth, therefore, a rest," — or, to render it more literally, I am told, " there remaineth, therefore, a Sabbath-keeping to the people of God " — and then he goes on to tell what it is ; to show that it is a spiritual rest. This seems to be the drift of his argument. The objector says, if you are right, then we have no Sabbath any more ; but he returns, Oh no, there still remains a Sabbath-keeping for the people of God ; that is, a Sabbath-keeping of the spirit, a rest in the soul and spirit of man, and not merely in the outward work ; a rest still remaining to those who are on the firm basis of truth and right. That is the Sabbath which he recognizes. Those have entered into this rest, who have passed from the letter which killeth, to the spirit which giveth life; they have entered into the Sabbath which remaineth for the people of God. If Paul could not give any other answer than this, it is because he did not know of any other Sabbath than this. And if he did not know of any other, it is not likely that he observed any other.

But I am taking up a great portion of the time, and will merely sum up what I have said in a few words.

FIRST — The institution of the Sabbath, alleged to have been given at the creation, could not have been thus instituted according to the letter, interpreted by the light of science.

SECOND — The institution of the Sabbath is a peculiarly Jewish institution, intended only for that people.

THIRD — The day and manner of its observance were widely different from that now inculcated for the first day of the week.

FOURTH — There is no evidence of any transfer of the obligation from the seventh to the first day, or to any day of the week.

FINALLY — By the testimony of the whole record of the New Testament, we are taught that now religion is to be regarded as a life, and not as a ceremony — as a spirit and a truth, and not a worship in the temple of Jerusalem, or in Mount Gerizim — that its ceremonies were but the shadow, which is lost to sight by the coming of the sunbeams before whose rays it was cast.

Stephen S. Foster next addressed the assembly, as follows:

In the results that have been presented to this Convention, and the remarks that have been made by those who have preceded me, considerable stress has been laid upon the statute laws requiring the observance of the Sabbath day, in distinction from other days of the week. I do not know that too much stress has been laid upon this, but to my mind it is a thing of little consequence. I do not regard these penal enactments as of any force, or their repeal as any moral gain to the cause of freedom. It may be well enough to have them re-

7*

pealed, and if anything can be accomplished by their repeal, I think it can be easily done; and for one, I should have no objection to petitioning for their repeal. Still, I think we should lose by it as much as we should gain. These penal enactments are sometimes of very great service to our cause, and these cases are when the attempt is made to enforce them.

Suppose, Mr. Chairman, that they should be enforced; the consequences are very trifling indeed. It is easy for you or me to lose a few dollars, or to spend a few hours, or days, or even weeks, in a prison. It does not injure us in the least as men. It has done us, as individuals, no harm. We are what we should have been, in all essential respects, had these enactments never been enforced or executed upon us. I do not look upon this as important. The loss of a few dollars, nay of all, what is it? Property is something that can be easily acquired. If it is gone, we can easily supply its place, or we can dispense with it. Property and personal freedom are, to my mind, of comparatively little consequence; but, Mr. Chairman, there is an injury done by the prevalent view of the Sabbath to this community, which is irreparable. It is the effect upon the immortal mind, of the sentiment which prevails, not in regard to punishing the violaters of the Sabbath, but in regard to the Sabbath itself. It is that which I most deplore. I have felt its sad consequences in my own person. I was trained to believe that the Sabbath was a holy day. How I came to believe it, I don't know, but suppose it was like other boys; I was accustomed to believe what my venerated mother told me, and what my minister told me. Such were my superstitious notions of this day, that I thought it a very great sin to take up an axe, and cut a stick of wood, but I could lift my foot a dozen times to break it. The sound of the axe must not be heard upon the Sabbath.

These notions followed me for years, and their sad effects were felt in almost every duty I was called to perform. For many years, when I stood upon the banks of the stream, to bathe in the pure and liquid fountain of health and peace, it was long before I could make up my mind to enter upon that most delightful duty, because my mother had told me of the many

instances of boys being drowned by going into the water on
Sunday; and I was really and positively afraid that I should be
drowned, because such was the effect of superstition upon my
mind, that I had not the absolute control of my limbs; and it
was not until many attempts, that I ventured out into the deep.
I mention this as a specimen of the dreadful influence of the
superstitious notions of the Sabbath day, which are everywhere taught. It is that which I deprecate, and not the taking
of a few paltry dollars, by the bigoted neighbor of mine, who
may choose to enforce the law. It is the effect upon our character, intellect, and moral nature, which is to be deplored; and
it is the cause of that effect which this Convention ought to
hold up to the contempt, and ridicule, and indignation of an
enlightened community.

This notion of the Sabbath, Sir, is the great capital of the
priesthood,—their only capital. It is that alone in which they
can traffic. It is that upon which their whole order rests. It
is their play-day,—the day upon which they perform. It is
that fact, that makes the day the "sun of the moral universe,"
in the estimation of the venerable Dr. Beecher. It is the day,
Mr. Chairman, the radiance of which gives them their bread,
and therefore they cling to it with more tenacity than they cling
to any other precept of the Bible, admitting that to be one. But
did Jesus Christ ever say a word against Sabbath-breakers as
sinners? He spoke against adulterers, and thieves, and liars,
and profane swearers, but did he ever speak against Sabbath-
breaking? Did the Apostles ever speak of Sabbath-breaking?
Not in a solitary instance; and yet if you go to meeting, (I
used to do such things, Mr. Chairman,) one half of all the denunciations of the priesthood are against Sabbath-breaking;
and they have got up a special society for the purpose of promoting the better observance of the Sabbath. Strange over-
sight in the Son of God! What a pity that the venerable Dr.
Beecher had not lived in his day, and called up that subject,
and asked him if he had not a word of denunciation for the
Sabbath-breaker!

This notion, that is disseminated from more than forty thousand pulpits in this country, that the Sabbath is a holy day, is a proposition most absurd and ridiculous. What is holiness? Is it the attribute of time, or the attribute of a thing? I had always supposed that holiness was an attribute of intelligence, that holiness and intelligence were inseparably connected, and that holiness could not be connected with anything but intelligence. If we were to speak of a holy horse, or a holy ox, a holy barn, or a holy stove, would it not shock the moral sense of every individual in this house? Is holiness the attribute of a thing, the attribute of matter, the attribute of place, the attribute of space, or the attribute of time? or is it the attribute of intelligence? Sir, the idea of holy time is an absurdity. God is holy; man is holy or unholy, because he is a moral, intelligent, and accountable being. But it is an attribute that cannot, in any sense, way, or shape, be applied to time. All time is the same. The sun shines; the wind blows; the trees wave their tops; the rocks look solemn in their eternal beds; vegetation springs forth under the radiance of the sun; all things move on the same, on Sunday as on Monday. There is no change; there is nothing in the whole circuit of nature to indicate that that day is in the slightest possible degree different from other days. There is nothing from which you could gather that God had distinguished it in the least from other days.

The only place wherein you can find anything like a distinction, is in the old Jewish law. But if you take the Sabbath of the Jews, then you must take the day which the Jews kept, and you must take it for the purposes for which it was established by the Jews; you must keep it as the Jews kept it, and you must punish its violations as the Jews punished it. Ah, Mr. Chairman, if the Jewish law of the Sabbath was executed, we should see all our priesthood swinging upon the gibbet to-morrow morning. There is not a man of them, that does not violate it every week. Not one of them keeps it, or pretends to keep it, for the purposes for which it was established by Moses. What was it established for? Purely as a day of rest. Every one was to lie still, and it was as much for the beast as for the man, just as much for the ox as for his owner. Every living thing was to rest, and lie still on that day. There was to be no harnessing of the horse to go off to meeting. That was a crime sending the owner of the horse to the gibbet—was it not? I appeal to your knowledge of that law; if a man had harnessed his animal, and driven him off five miles to attend a meeting, would they not have stoned him to death? Yet we are told now, that we must do it, or go to hell; there is no alternative.

Our friend, (Mr. Burleigh,) who has preceded me, has reasoned this matter very ably. I cannot do it. I cannot make an argument in favor of the non-observance of the Sabbath day. I have not the language, I have not the patience to do it. I want to argue against something, but our friend has the very happy faculty of arguing against nothing at all, and making a very profound, able, and interesting argument. But I ask our friend, if he does not feel that he has argued against nothing, after all? The "sacredness of the Sabbath"—who believes, or who ever thought of such a thing? No man of sense; little boys, old men, and old women, that never think for themselves, think there is something sacred about the Sabbath. The boys disbelieve it, because it only wants to be told them, and they know it at once. The only thing it is necessary for this Convention to do, it seems to me, except to occupy the time, and amuse and interest those here, is simply to assert the fact that there is no Sabbath, and everybody will know it. You don't need to argue, for there is no argument to it. I have no patience to reason or talk about the Sabbath. There is no Sabbath. It is all a humbug and delusion. All days are alike. Everything keeps on one day as on another. All time is alike. If you spend a day profitably to yourself and your fellow-men, you will have kept it holy; you will have been holy through the day. I will assert these facts, and there I will leave it. I hope this Convention will send out a strong voice, through the length and breadth of the land, saying to the children and youth, "THERE IS NO SABBATH; there are no holy days; all days are alike; and all men are holy, who do their duty to God and their fellow-men."

One thing more I would do. I would set the example to children, of doing on Sunday what I do on other days. If I make hay on Saturday, I make it on Sunday. I may be tired and glad to rest, but my neighbors do not make it on Sunday, and I feel it my duty to do it. When my neighbors get so that they are not afraid to make hay on Sunday, and then choose to meet together, I may be glad to meet with them. I wish to show that I can do this, and yet live. My barns have not yet been burned, although there is considerable hay in them that was got in on Sunday. You may tell Dr. Edwards, that a man can do this, and not be struck with lightning. I have got them insured, but the Insurance Company seemed not to be entire converts to this faith; for they did not charge me any extra per centage that I know of. I am inclined to think that this doctrine of Dr. Edwards is not gaining ground, although I have no doubt that he is exerting himself to the utmost. I think the best teacher is example. So long as the community think it to be wrong to work on Sunday, I shall feel it my duty to work on Sunday. But when it shall be generally understood that there is no distinction in days, then, if convenient, I shall be very glad to lay it aside. I don't like the idea of working seven days in the week. A man who will work half the time, ought to have a good living. But I do think, in the present state of society, we can preach most effectually, especially to children and youth, by going about our ordinary employments. If you don't like to work all day, work half the day, and be sure to work where you will be seen. Show them that you can work on Sunday, and yet not cheat on Monday. I think the good sense of this community will be satisfied that it is better to work on Sunday, and be honest all the time, than to keep the Sunday, and lie, cheat, and steal, the remaining six days of the week.

Mr. Foster was followed by Parker Pillsbury, who said:—

It would, perhaps, be better to continue the train of remark which has been commenced this evening, but there are one or two other things, upon which I wish to say a few words. I wish to notice the manner in which the Sabbath is regarded in the Vermont Chronicle of yesterday's date; and the Chronicle is the organ of Congregational Christianity in that State. I find in it a little article, headed, "WAR AND THE SABBATH," that I regard as a very striking illustration of the manner in which the Sabbath is held and observed by the Orthodox Christianity of the country. The article begins with quoting from another paper an account of a military inspection of the brigade under the command of General Cushing, on Sunday, which it considers as a violation of the day. A *march* is perfectly in keeping with the day, I suppose, for the soldiers marched from Matamoras to Monterey, some fifty or sixty miles, on the Sabbath; but that, I suppose, was only a "Sabbath day's journey," and no violation of the sacredness of the day! A *battle*, also, is in perfect keeping with the requirements of God in regard to the Sabbath. The slaughter of an army is no sin, but to review an army violates the Sabbath! The storming of Monterey was carried on on Sunday; the surrender of Vera Cruz also took place on Sunday. These, however, were perfectly in accordance with the law of the Sabbath; for I hear of no religious paper which has ever deprecated either of these transactions; and yet both of them were accompanied with immense slaughter, not only of American soldiery, but of Mexican women and children. There was no sin in the storming of Monterey on Sunday, but to review General Cushing's regiment was a violation of the Sabbath!

This afternoon, Mr. Parker alluded to the fact, that some kinds of theological preaching were in perfect keeping with the Sabbath. While all defence of the rights of man, or the drunkard, was in violation of the day, a Congregational clergyman could preach eight Sundays in succession, in defence of the doctrine of infant baptism, when some of his church members had become somewhat heretical upon that point; and this was regarded as excellent keeping of the Sabbath. The same clergyman preached a sermon, in which he defined what was and what was not proper on the first day of the week. Among other things, he said that, on their way to or from church, if they were addressed by a neighbor or friend, they were under no obligation whatever to return any answer; and he would suggest to them that they pass each other in silence on the first day of the week, and if addressed by a stranger or friend, that they should return no answer. This is the kind of Sabbath-keeping proclaimed in our community. In regard to this eight Sundays' preaching about infant baptism, I know of not a single instance in which that minister has ever uttered one breath against the act of infant butchery, which has been carried on in Mexico for the last twenty-four months. To slaughter infants by the hundred, as they have been slaughtered in Mexico, is no crime; the minister of that church has not lifted his voice against it; but not to baptize an infant is a crime of such magnitude as to deserve the spending of eight Sundays in succession.

I wished to make a remark upon the earnestness as well as the intelligence, apparent in the audience to-day, and this evening, which are to me most cheering indications. I believe that if the clergy understood the deep feeling there is in the community, in relation to the Sabbath, they would be far more solicitous than they now are. Nearly one-half of their preaching is in regard to the Sabbath. But there is a mighty undercurrent of feeling, and the calling of this Convention is, I believe, the precursor of a far more desirable state of things. It was well remarked this afternoon, [by Mr. Alcott,] that our books are kept by clerks; we employ men to do for us everything of a moral and religious nature. Our repenting and our praying are done by proxy; our religion is mainly carried on by proxy. There has been a mistake among the community, that there is no necessity of our making use of the powers and faculties God has given us. We do not aspire to be anything but what our fathers were, and are satisfied to tread in their footsteps. They have been Whigs, and we must be Whigs; or they have been Democrats, and we must be Democrats. Whigs look upon young men as so much stock in trade to be manufactured into Whigs. Democrats take a similar view; and young men become perfectly reconciled to it, and look upon themselves as only material, lumber if you please, to be

worked up into politicians. The ministry takes a similar
view of the rising generation. What is the intention of the
Sabbath School? Is it anything more or less than a manufac-
tory of sectarians? What are our Sunday schools, but West
Point institutions for the education of spiritual cadets for the
sectarianism of the country? It takes mighty little to make a
politician; it takes very little to make a Baptist, and next to
nothing to make a Methodist. The idea that only God could
create out of nothing has been almost superseded; sectarians
and politicians are made out of next to nothing, if not altogether nothing. People look upon themselves as a great
lumber-yard, piled up with lumber, to be hewed out into politicians and sectarians. It is a shame to the generation, a
reproach to the age, that the young men have no higher and
holier aspirations.

A theological student said that he loved Thanksgiving day,
and Fast day, but he could not say he loved the Sabbath. It
is not until they come out into the community, and find the
Sabbath a harvest-day, that they fall in love with it. You
know you have no love for the day; why not dare to speak
your convictions? You go to meeting on Sunday, and hear
your minister talk very large, and long, and loud, about the
heroism of Christianity:

> "Should earth against my soul engage,
>   And hellish darts be hurled,
> Still I can smile at Satan's rage,
>   And face a frowning world;"—

and yet that minister dare not face his nearest neighbor, nor
you either! You know that you do not love the Sabbath, but
dare not say it.

I am glad of the calling of this Convention, and the multitude it has brought together. I trust that it will increase in
numbers and interest up to its very close, and that to-day shall
be but the beginning of a revolution that shall eclipse, far
eclipse, the revolution in France, which at this moment is
rocking all nations. This is not to be a trifling matter. The

Sabbath is the forlorn hope of the Church, and never will be given up without a great struggle. It is the Gibraltar of sectarian worship. You are all tired of it, but you dare not brave public opinion.

Friend Foster mentioned the burning of barns and upsetting of boats, urged by the pulpit in defence of the Sabbath. No doubt, there are more accidents in proportion on the Sabbath. You are cowards; you expect to be drowned, and therefore you are drowned; and your cowardice is the occasion of it. God don't go about drowning folks on Sunday. God is no incendiary to set fire to folks's barns, and burn their hay and cattle. It is your own cowardice. Go into the water, cool, calm, and composed, and you come out safe. Go trembling, and expecting that God is upon your track to drown you, and you will probably be drowned. If you sincerely believe you ought to keep the Sabbath, go and keep it. I hold you responsible; you are a Sabbath-breaker if you do not. But I am not to be judged by your conscience. I hold you to the doctrine of the New Testament: "Whatsoever is not of faith is sin; and he that doubts is damned"—and you damn yourselves by your doubts.

You all know that the argument for the Sabbath rests upon the Bible. I stand ready to prove to the clergy, out of their own mouths, that whether the Bible teach the doctrine or not, it does not help the matter at all; for there is not a theological seminary but admits to the world that its authority is, after all, a piece of deception which they practise upon the people, and that they have no belief themselves in its authority.

The discussion was further continued by Wm. Lloyd Garrison, and James N. Buffum, of Lynn, in support of the resolutions; and at 10 o'clock,

Adjourned to meet at 9 1-2 o'clock, to-morrow morning.

Friday Morning.

Convention met agreeably to adjournment, the President in the Chair.

S. S. Foster moved that all persons be allowed to participate in the discussions of this Convention. Discussed with much earnestness, and at considerable length, by Richard Thayer, S. S. Foster, Wm. L. Garrison, I. S. Smith, G. W. F. Mellen, G. W. Benson, and Henry C. Wright. Negatived.

The resolutions before the Convention, at the time of adjournment, were taken up for discussion.

Henry C. Wright spoke as follows :—

I wish to make a few suggestions, with regard to some of the topics brought forward in the resolutions offered yesterday. I do not now call to mind any specific resolution, and will, therefore, speak to the general question. The point at issue between us and our opponents is this,—*the divine right and obligation of the first-day Sabbath.* Those who were present yesterday, I think, must have been powerfully impressed with the argument of our friend Burleigh, touching the Scripture authority on this subject. My own view is this. I do not ask what the Jewish Scriptures say upon the subject. I go to the Christian Scriptures, and there I find the Sabbatical observance classed with the rudiments of the world and its beggarly elements, and a distinct injunction upon Christians not to judge one another touching times and places. I find a strict injunction, that we are not to enforce upon one another the observance of Sabbaths and new moons. The whole tenor of the New Testament, and of the Christian religion, is to abolish the observance of times and places. Christianity is not a religion of time and place. I start with that position—CHRISTIANITY IS NOT A RELIGION OF TIME AND PLACE. It is an all-pervading, omnipresent principle of life. It knows no such thing as holy places, holy times, holy garments, holy church organizations, or holy constitutions of national organizations. It knows no such thing as sanctifying days; it sanctifies human beings. It never speaks a word of consecrating times and places to God, and we challenge Sabbatarians to show that it does. They never have discussed the question; they dare not. We know that there is no such thing in the Christian religion, as the consecration of time and place to God; but it does consecrate men and women to Him.

Why should we talk about sacred times and places? What do Sabbatarians mean by consecrating *time* to God? If they mean anything besides consecrating *men*, let them say so. If that is what you mean, there is not a man nor a woman in this Convention, who would not cordially unite with you. But why not use correct language in this matter, if this is *all* you mean? Why talk about consecrating a *day*, when we mean consecrating *ourselves?* I care not what becomes of the day. Let us only consecrate ourselves, and the day will take care of itself, whether Sunday or Monday.

Now, Sir, this whole community, from Andover to Princeton, from the Penobscot to the Gulf of Mexico,—all over this nation, the church and the clergy are devoting their time to consecrating a day, but seem to care nothing about consecrating human beings; for these very men are making merchandize of their brethren, and shaking hands with those who do so. As the Vermont Chronicle seems to say, it is right to fight battles and butcher *men* on the Sabbath, but you must consecrate the *day* to God! It is very difficult for me to respect the honesty or motives of such men, who seem to care nothing about men, but everything about a day. Christ tells us to keep ourselves holy; and why should we talk about keeping a day holy? We have a great Sabbatical institution in this nation, and what is its object? Not to induce men to keep themselves holy—they do not talk about that; it is about keeping a day holy. And how will you do that? Give us the philosophy of the thing. Give us the rationale of it. I cannot understand the thing, under the Christian dispensation. I can understand it, under the Jewish dispensation; for in the Old Testament, keeping the day holy was simply consecrating it to rest from labor, and nothing else. There is no such thing there, as consecrating a day to religious observances and exercises.

There is nothing in the Bible about consecrating a day to the worship of God. There is nothing in nature about it.

There is a fallacy about this matter. People go about their business for six days in the week, but God is not in their thoughts at all; moral obligations are not in their thoughts. They give themselves up to the indulgence of their passions, their avarice and ambition; they go headlong in their career, until the hands on the dial-plate point to a particular hour of a particular day, and then they must begin to be holy! They must stop their worldly business, their *secular* affairs, and must begin to look after *holy* affairs, and spiritual business! They must stop looking after their bodies, and begin to look after their souls! They who have been cheating men all the week, —who have been making merchandize of men, or butchering men,—as soon as the hands on the dial get to a particular point, stop; and now what are they going to do? To begin to worship God!

They go to meeting in the morning on Sunday; the great congregation comes before the minister, and he gravely gets up, and gravely utters it to the people, with a solemn voice and look—"Let us begin to worship God." What had they been worshipping before? I ask the question, because I want to show the absurdity of that expression; but how truly it tells the character of the religion of this country! "Let us begin the worship of God." How? By letting the oppressed go free? No. By doing justice and loving mercy? No. By restoring four-fold for the wrong you have done? No. By repenting of your evil deeds? No. By paying every man his just dues? No. By the consecration of yourselves to God? No. And how then? Why, "BY SINGING THE FOLLOWING PSALM." That is the way they are going to begin to worship God; just as if He who sits upon His eternal throne, the All-pervading Spirit of the universe, was to be pleased and profited by the singing of a psalm or a hymn! They do not sing their psalm to benefit themselves; it is to please the Deity—as though He was to be gratified with the sound of the organ, the fiddle and the flute, and all that music which is made in the gallery! I like music. I am exceedingly fond of it, and have no objections to anybody's singing, at any time and any place, in all God's universe. Sing as much as you please. But don't tell me, when it is half past ten, or quarter before eleven o'clock, to begin now to worship God, by singing the following psalm or hymn. Then you go on with your singing, read a chapter in the Bible, say a prayer or two, and have a sermon, and then the minister gets up and says, "LET US CONCLUDE THE WORSHIP OF GOD"—and how? "By singing the following psalm." And there the worship of God is begun and ended, all crowded into about an hour and a half; and the people go out of the meeting-house, like boys out of school, glad to get away.

Thus it is; the worship of the Almighty is a mere matter of time and place, a mere matter of observance and ceremony, with us in this day and in this nation, as really and truly as it is with the Mohammedan, who, at a particular hour of the day, drops upon his knee with his face towards Mecca, or with any other people who go through with similar forms.

I have a little incident taken from the Eutaw (Alabama) Whig, in which there is an advertisement, that, on Friday, on such a day of last December, at such a place, and at such an hour, would commence the sale of one hundred and sixty negroes, forty-seven mules, one hundred and forty pork-hogs and stock-hogs, with a certain number of old carts and wagons, and plantation tools, at auction. The sale went on during Friday and Saturday, and all was perfectly right. Your Boston Recorders, your New England Puritans, your Vermont Chronicles, your New York Observers, and your religious papers all over the land, had not a word to say against it. That is only the desecration of *men* — selling men at auction; they cannot notice that transaction. Their business is, not to look after men, but to look after the Sabbath. If they will only carry on this traffic in the bodies and souls of men on the lawful days of the week, during Friday and Saturday, the religious papers, the churches and the clergy, have nothing to say about it. But, as soon as it came to Saturday night, and the hands pointed the hour of twelve, then the business was all stopped. The negroes and cattle that remained unsold, were all driven into a pen, and locked up, to be kept there over Sunday. The people that were selling and buying those human beings, being good Methodists, Baptists and Presbyterians,—all very pious people, for they had been having a revival in that vicinity,—could not sell those human beings on Sunday. That would be horrible! Not to sell human beings, but to sell them on *that day!* It would not desecrate the man, but it would desecrate a certain day. They, therefore, locked them up, and went to their churches. They began to worship God, not by opening the pen to let those creatures go free, but by singing psalms, muttering over prayers, and hearing sermons. They carried on their worship during Sunday, and as soon as Sunday was over, according to the advertisement which said that the sale would be continued on Monday, they went on with the sale of the negroes, and mules, and hogs, the remainder of what had been advertised to be sold.

Had these persons, engaged in the traffic of human beings, continued the sale during Sunday, they would have been turned out of the church; not for desecrating men,—oh, no! that is not their mission, they are too holy for that,—but for desecrating a day. "Desecrate a day," "break a day," "break a Sabbath"—I do wish the people would learn to look into the philosophy and rationale of certain phrases floating in this community. They may break necks by the thousand, but they cannot break a day. They may tear human bodies to pieces, but, oh! do not break a day. I sincerely wish that all the hanging in this nation had to be done in front of the pulpits on the Sabbath, and that ministers had to do it. I wish you would petition your Legislature to compel your ministers to do it, if they will plead for the gallows. They plead for the breaking of human necks; but, oh! do not break the Sabbath. They may tear men, women, and children to pieces, but must be careful to keep a day sacred; and so, by keeping up that delusion of sacred days, they compensate, in the estimation of mankind, for their butchery of human beings. "Pure religion and undefiled before God is, to visit the widows and the fatherless in their affliction, and to keep unspotted from the world"; but pure religion and undefiled, according to the definition of the churches of this nation, is to keep the Sabbath, to go to meeting, and to go through certain observances.

If I were to go forth into this nation, as the agent of the American and Foreign Sabbath Union, for the purpose of rescuing a day from desecration, and should come to Boston, there is not a pulpit in the city but would admit me. The Old South, the Park street, Bowdoin street, Essex street, and Winter street, would welcome me. Every church would welcome me. But let me come to the city as the agent of a society, whose mission is, to rescue MAN from the desecration of the auction-block, from the gallows, and the battle-field, and there is scarcely a church in the city which I could get to speak in.

Is it the mission of Christianity to look after days, or after men? The Sabbatarian principle says, that the great business of Christianity is to consecrate the Sabbath; the anti-Sabbatarian principle is, to consecrate man; and that is where we differ. I want to place it upon that position, and meet our opponents there. Rev. Justin Edwards, and all his compeers, are preaching and praying about the consecration of a day. We preach and pray for the consecration of man.

"ANTI-SABBATARIAN"! I glory in the name. There is no one day Sabbath in the Christian religion. We have no holy boards, or holy nails, or holy iron, or holy stoves, or holy titles, but only holy men and holy women. Is man an appendage to the Sabbath, or is the Sabbath an appendage to man? They would hold up the idea, that God looks after the institution, and not after men; and they tell us that he comes forth with all the thunderbolts of heaven, with earthquakes, plagues and diseases, to take care of a day; he hurls all the thunderbolts and plagues upon man, because he violates the Sabbath.

We might say, upon this principle, that God institutes a hat for the good of the head; the hat is a divine ordinance, a divine institution; and then he knocks out the brains to save the hat. A holy hat! The brains and the head are nothing; the hat is everything, and so God looks after the hat. I buy a coat for the good of the body. It is a sacred coat, a holy coat, a God-ordained coat, a sanctified coat; and now my great business is to consecrate the coat to God, no matter what becomes of the body or the soul. The head must be sacrificed to the hat; the man to the institution; the substance to the shadow.

There is a great Sabbatarian Union in England, Scotland, France, and Germany; all Christendom is moving for a great *Sabbath* Alliance. And is it their object to look after man? No, Sir! The very men who compose that Sabbath Alliance are among the most desperate robbers, tyrants, and murderers on the earth: the American slaveholders take the lead in it! Their object is not to look after man; but it is agitating the religious sentiment of the whole land to consecrate the coat, the hat, the garments to God. They care nothing about souls and bodies; their business is to guard the institution, the dress, the outward form. Look at the Sabbath Manual, put forth by Justin Edwards; it tells how God looks after the Sabbath, and not how he looks after men; how he instituted the Sabbath for the good of man, and then slaughters for the sake of the Sabbath! Can such folly be attributable to God? No.

I hold in my hand an article from the New England Puritan, upon the Sabbath cause at the South. Rev. Justin Edwards, the Secretary and General Agent of the American and Foreign Sabbath Union, has been travelling through the South, collecting money to keep the Sabbath holy. He has been among the SLAVEHOLDERS, to get them to combine in this great movement. The very men whose hands are steeped in blood, who live by breeding and selling human beings, these are the men who compose the Sabbath Union. Justin Edwards had not a word to say about remembering man to keep him holy. Had he uttered such a sentence in the ears of the South, they would have treated him as they treated the agent of Massachusetts, the venerable Mr. Hoar. They would have despatched him at once from their borders, and given him a walking ticket. Had he said a word about consecrating or desecrating man, depend upon it, Justin Edwards would have come home with all speed;

but he spoke of keeping the Sabbath—the whole South opened their arms to receive him, because they supposed that, by keeping a day holy, they could compensate for the horrible business in which they are engaged, of desecrating humanity.

[He concluded his remarks by reading the letter of Justin Edwards, and commenting upon it; and took his seat, after expressing the hope that Lucretia Mott, of Philadelphia, would next address the meeting.]

Lucretia Mott, of Philadelphia, addressed the Convention as follows: —

I have little to add to what has been already said upon this subject. Much that I could not have spoken so well, has been said for me by others. I am glad to be here, to have an opportunity of hearing the discussions, and also to give countenance to this important movement for the progress of the religious world. The distinction has been clearly and ably drawn, between mere forms and rituals of the Church, and practical goodness; between the consecration of man, and the consecration of days, the dedication of the Church, and the dedication of our lives to God.

But might we not go further, and shew that we are not to rely so much upon books, even upon the Bible itself, as upon the higher revelation within us? The time is come, and especially in New England is it come, that man should judge of his own self what is right, and that he should seek authority less from the Scriptures. It is well, however, inasmuch as the faith of a large part of the professors of Christianity rests upon this book, to shew that certain also of their own teachers bear witness to the truth we advocate.

It seemed to me that the views of the last speaker went further to sanctify the book, than his own principles would justify. I thought the same of the remarks of Theodore Parker, made yesterday, with regard to the day, and wished to allude to it in his presence, but there was no opportunity. There seemed to be a little confusion, when he spoke of not hallowing the day, and yet considered it essential that there should be this religious observance. Does not such an admission lead the advo-

cates of it into a kind of compromise? and to "build again
that which they are called to destroy"? It is observable, in
nearly all the advance steps in theological points, particularly
when there is a reluctance to acknowledge the heresy, and a
desire to appear orthodox.

Those who differ from us would care little for an Anti-
Sabbath Convention, which should come to the conclusion
that, after all, it would be best to have one day in seven set
apart for religious purposes. Few intelligent clergymen will
now admit, that they consecrate the day in any other sense, or
that there is any inherent holiness in it. If you should agree
that this day should be ·for more holy purposes than other
days, you have granted much that they ask. Is not this Convention prepared to go farther than this? to dissent from this
idea, and declare openly, that it is lawful to do good on the
Sabbath day? That it is the consecration of all our ·time to
God and to goodness, that is required of us? Not by demure
piety; not by avoiding innocent recreation on any day of the
week; but by such a distribution of time as shall give sufficient
opportunity for such intellectual culture and spiritual improvement, as our mental and religious nature requires. There
would not then be the necessity of a devotion of the seventh
part of our time, even for the rational improvement that our
friend yesterday considered so essential.

In the Scripture authority, however, as it has been cited, it
might have been shown, that, even in the times of the most
rigid Jewish observance, it was regarded as a shadow only of
good things to come. "I gave them also my Sabbaths to be a
sign unto them." The distinction was then made, by the more
faithful and discerning of their people, between mere formal
worship and practical goodness. "Lord, who shall abide in
thy tabernacle? who shall dwell in thy holy hill? He that
walketh uprightly, and worketh righteousness, and speaketh
the truth in his heart." When these things were not done,
even the temple-worship became an abomination; the Sabbaths, the holy meetings, he was weary of them. Their clear-
sighted prophets spoke in the name of the Highest, to those

who had violated the law of right: "I hate, I despise your
feast-days. The new moons and Sabbaths, the calling of
assemblies, I cannot away with; it is iniquity, even the solemn
meeting." They were called to amend their ways and their
doings — to do justly, love mercy, and walk humbly. There
is now, as there ever has been, but one test — one standard of
true worship.

If we were better acquainted with the doctrines and principles of the ancients, of those who are not regarded as coming
within any divine enclosure, but who are looked upon as heathen, we should find abundant recognition of practical Christianity. Who is it that tells us that the testimony of a Socra-
tes is not equally corroborative of truth, with the testimony of
a Paul? That certain authorities, bound in a certain way, are
of higher credence, than that which has come through other
channels? Man is man, and his rational and spiritual natures
are worthy of respect. His testimony is corroborative in every
age of the world, let it come from what source it may, while in
accordance with truth.

It has been said here, that we are not bound by the Old
Testament; but are we to bind ourselves to the New Testament authority? Enough has already been quoted from that
book, to prove all that we would ask, with regard to the day.
There is no testimony, no evidence there found, that will authorize the consecration of one day above another. Jesus
recognized no such distinction; and the Apostle Paul said,
"Let every man be fully persuaded in his own mind. He that
regardeth the day, unto the Lord he doth regard it; and he that
regardeth not the day, unto the Lord he doth not regard it."
These equally give God thanks. There is all this liberal view,
and it is well to bring it before the people. But, after all, are
we to take this as our sufficient authority? Suppose some of
them had been so under their Jewish prejudices, as to teach
the importance of the observance of the day; would that have
made it obligatory on us? No, we are not called to follow im-
plicitly any outward authority. Suppose that Jesus himself
had said, with regard to the day, as he did in allusion to John's

baptism, "Suffer it to be so now," would that have made it binding on us? Is the example of the ancients, whether Prophets or Apostles, or the "beloved Son of God" himself, sufficient for the entire regulation of our action at the present day? No: Jesus testified to his disciples, that when the spirit of truth was come, they should be taught all things, and should do the things which he did, and greater. The people were not then prepared for more. The time would come when that which was spoken in the ear, in closets, should be proclaimed on the house-top. He urged upon his disciples to keep their eye single, that their whole body might be full of light.

His practice, then, in any of these observances, is not sufficient authority for us. We are not required to walk in the exact path of our predecessors, in any of our steps through life. We are to conform to the spirit of the present age, to the demand of the present life. Our progress is dependant upon our acting out our convictions. New bottles for new wine now, as in days past. Let us not be ashamed of the gospel that we profess, so far as to endeavor to qualify it with any orthodox ceremonies or expressions. We must be willing to stand out in our heresy; especially, as already mentioned, when the duty of Sabbath observance is carried to such an extent, that it is regarded, too generally, a greater crime to do an innocent thing on the first day of the week,—to use the needle, for instance,—than to put a human being on the auction-block on the second day;—a greater crime to engage in harmless employment on the first day, than to go into the field of battle, and slay our fellow-beings, either on that or other days of the week! While there is this palpable inconsistency, it is demanded of us, not only to speak plainly, but to act out our convictions, and not seem to harmonize with the religious world generally, when our theory is not in accordance with theirs.

Many religionists apparently believe that they are consecrating man to the truth and the right, when they convert him to their creeds—to their scheme of salvation, and plan of redemption. They, therefore, are very zealous for the traditions of their fathers, and for the observance of days; while at the same time, as already mentioned, they give countenance to war, slavery, and other evils; not because they are wholly reckless of the condition of man, but because such is their sectarian idea. Their great error is in imagining that the highest good is found in their church. Hence their zeal and proselyting spirit.

The religious world ought to be disabused of this idea, and made to understand the real consecration of time. In order to do this, not only should this Convention be held, and resolutions, urging the carrying out of our principles, be passed; but we should be prepared to issue tracts, and scatter them over the land. This has been done, to some extent. There are several copies here, of a tract published a year or two ago in Philadelphia, on this question, by one, who, not feeling qualified to write, spoke to his friend who could write, but had not the means to publish, and agreed to furnish the means. This is the right kind of zeal, leading to individual labor, not mere conventional interest. The more is it called for, on account of the extraordinary efforts in holding Sabbath Conventions, &c. Men of talents and reputed religious worth are going about the country, making exertions to establish a Sabbath, to increase its obligations, and the necessity of its observance, on the part of the people.

The editors of some of the daily papers in Philadelphia, especially since the issue of the Anti-Sabbath Call, are catering to the religious sentiment, praising the labors of Edwards and others, in travelling about for this purpose. In proportion as these publications go forth, should there be zeal on the part of the Anti-Sabbatarians, as they are called by way of distinction, to spread clear, intelligent, and liberal views on the subject. There should, therefore, be a generous appropriation of means and funds to circulate information, and to enlighten the people, and a reasonable portion of our time and talents devoted to the cause. The reformer should advocate a portion of every day of the week, for mental and spiritual improvement, as well as innocent recreation, rather than give sanction to the idea, that the present arrangement is a wise distribution of our time.

In the existing state of society, while the laborer is over-tasked, and has so little respite from his toil, we may indeed rejoice, that, by common consent, he has even this one day in seven of rest; when if he choose, he ought to be encouraged to go out with his family, in steamboats and railroad cars; and in the fields and woods he might offer acceptable homage and worship to the Highest. This exercise of his right need not interfere at all with the conscientious action of those, who believe they may more acceptably worship God in temples made with hands. But if we take the ground, that all should rather assemble on that day, to worship, and hear what is called religious instruction, there is danger of our yielding the very point for which we are called together.

Many of us verily believe that there is, on the whole, material harm done to the people, in these false observances, and in the dogmas which are taught as religious truth. So believing, we should endeavor to discourage this kind of devotion of the time, and correct these errors, by plain speaking and honest walking—rather than, by our example and our admissions, do that which shall go to strengthen superstition, and increase idolatry in the land.

C. C. Burleigh offered, in behalf of Charles K. Whipple, the following resolutions:—

Resolved, That the American and Foreign Sabbath Union be requested to furnish in their tracts, and in the public lectures of their agent, proof from the Bible of these two positions: 1st, That *God* requires of men *any* peculiar observance of *Sunday*; 2nd, That he requires them to observe it by attendance on meetings *conducted by clergymen*, and by *abstinence from labor and recreation* on the parts of the day not thus occupied.

Resolved, That the physical and moral welfare of the community would be greatly promoted by the running of trains of passenger-cars on Sunday, from city to country, and from country to city.

Adjourned to meet at half past 2 o'clock.

AFTERNOON SESSION.

Met pursuant to adjournment, the President in the chair.

Voted, That 4 o'clock be assigned as the time for taking the sense of the Convention on the resolutions under consideration.

Henry C. Wright, from the Business Committee, reported the subjoined resolutions, which were adopted:—

Resolved, That when this Convention adjourn, it adjourn to meet one year hence, in the city of Boston, New York, or Philadelphia, at such time and place as the Publishing Committee shall appoint.

Resolved, That a Committee of five be appointed by this Convention, to superintend the publication of its doings, and of such documents, relating to the subjects brought before it, as the Committee shall have the means to do—the Committee having power to decide what documents shall take precedence in publication.

The following persons were appointed on this committee, viz.: W. L. Garrison, Henry C. Wright, Francis Jackson, Charles K. Whipple, John W. Browne.

The discussion upon the resolutions before the Convention was resumed by C. C. Burleigh, as follows:—

It is not my purpose, this afternoon, to take up much of the time of the Convention—for a regard both to them and to myself would forbid my doing so; but there are some points presented in these resolutions, which have not been noticed, or have been touched upon but lightly, but which may be profitably considered for a brief space. What I have already said does not cover all the controversy between those who uphold, and those who disapprove of the observance of the first day of the week as peculiarly sacred. I endeavored to show, yesterday forenoon and evening, first, that even admitting the correctness of the Sabbatarian view of the first day of the week, the Legislature has no right to enforce the observance of the religious duties supposed to be enjoined in the Sabbatical law; and second, that when we make our appeal to the Scriptures of the Old and New Testaments, we find no reason for believing that the first day Sabbatarians are right in supposing that the first day of the week is any more sacred than the other days of the week; or that God has ever commanded man to observe the first day of the week; or that the Sabbatical institution we now hold to is identical in any essential points with that ordained for the Jews. I endeavored to show this, from the testimony of the very Scriptures to which the advocates of the Sabbath make their appeal. I further endeavored to show, that there is strong evidence against it; the evidence of the declarations and acts of Jesus and his apostles, which can by no fair rule of interpretation be reconciled with a belief in the peculiar sacredness of the first day of the week, as held and taught by Jesus and his apostles.

But we are told, in reply,—or, as they would say, in addition to their Scripture argument,—that the laws of physiology agree with what is claimed to be the law of revelation upon this point. We are told that it is necessary for the welfare of man and beast, that a rest-day, once in seven days, should occur. We glanced at that cursorily in the consideration of other points, but have not yet looked directly and distinctly at it; at least, while I have been in the house. The law of Physiology, it is said, requires rest from bodily labor one day in every seven; and why? Because continual toil wears out the system! Nobody denies that. We know that continual toil wears out the system; but we join issue with the advocates of a weekly day of rest, upon this point, that though one day in seven is better than no rest at all,—though it is better to abandon our common occupations, if toilsome, and devote ourselves to intellectual and moral occupations instead, giving repose to the body, and time to repair its wasted energies,—it would be still better to distribute the periods of labor and rest more evenly over the whole time.

We have two objections to the opinions of the Sabbatarians upon this point. First,—they do not duly discriminate among the different classes of society. Men toil in the field, in the work-shop, and in the study. The minister who goes into his library, and sits there during the six days of the week, if he is industrious, turns over the theological volumes, storing his mind with materials for his duties on the first day of the week. The farmer in the open field breathes the pure air of heaven as he drives· the plough, or wields the hoe, the scythe, or the sickle. By the time the week has come to its end, these two men are in very different positions. There is the sedentary class of men, and the class engaged in active bodily exercise. Now you want a rest, adapted to repair the wasted energies which these men have lost; and what sort of a rest? The Sabbatarian says to the farmer, "Put by the scythe, the plough, and the sickle." He says, in the intervals between the morning of the day, and the hour for the church, and after church to the evening of the day, he must retire to his own house, and study the Bible, read religious books, catechise the children, or converse upon religious topics, and only those.

I remember once that I was at the house of a clergyman, who was a strong believer in this doctrine. It chanced that I was to speak upon the subject of slavery in his meeting-house in the afternoon, for he did not carry his notions so far as to think it unlawful to preach righteousness and humanity on the Sabbath, although he believed in the observance of the Sabbath-day, and that right strictly. He preached that forenoon upon the observance of the Sabbath. He said, we must not think our own thoughts; we must not speak our own words, or do our own acts; we must engage in no secular conversation. On the first day of the week, all our talk must be of religion, all our thoughts of religion, everything which we permitted the mind to turn upon must have a view to religion—meaning thereby, religion in the narrow acceptation of the term—meaning theological religion, if I may use the phrase. Of course, I did not like to offend the man's feelings, or go across his prejudices in his own house, and so I was very careful not to say anything to go against his views. Before dinner was over, he had himself led the conversation to a great variety of topics, not one-third part of which would have come under his definition of religious subjects. So it seems that he was preaching a doctrine which neither he nor his congregation were able to

bear. Certainly, he did not bear it. This is the doctrine that
we must not think our own thoughts, speak our own words, or
do our own actions on the first day of the week, the day of
rest, or restraint from manual labor and bodily exercise.

I have, indeed, heard of a Doctor of Divinity,—I know not
whether the account is authentic or not,—who considers the
Sabbath the sun of the moral universe, and yet is so sensible of the necessity of bodily exercise for his constitution, that
he goes down cellar, and shovels sand from one side to the
other on the first day of the week. I believe that this inti-
mates a truth. Now, apply that to the case before us. Here
is a sedentary man, sitting in his closet all the week. His
business, his work, has been sitting still; and one would think
that the laws of Nature prescribed to him that he must change,
by going into the open air; that, instead of going down cellar to shovel sand, he should go out into the pure atmosphere; that he should go to the wood-pile, and chop wood, or
go into the garden, and dig with the spade or the hoe. But
the Sabbatical law makes no distinction in the two cases. It
says just as much to the sedentary man, to the lawyer, or the
minister, who sits in his closet during the week, to those who
are confined in the prosecution of their several callings whereby they earn their bread, as to the farmer who is employed
in the fields in manual labor, that they are to find their rest
in the house, and to turn their thoughts to religion or to religious books. Is that reasonable on the ground of physiology?
No help can be brought in from the Scriptures; they do not
require us to keep the day in the way that the Sabbatical laws
require us to keep it.

It might be very well, if the farmer and the mechanic had
labored so long as to have worn out their frames, so that the
rest of the night should be more than swallowed up by each
day's labor, and insufficient to restore full vigor and activity,—
it may be very well for such to rest from labor, to sit down
and meditate, or to enter into conversation with their neighbors upon suitable subjects, upon subjects which would be
suitable for any day of the week; it may be well to spend the

time in cultivating their highest nature, and raising their thoughts to their Maker with hopes and aspirations after a nobler life. But, looking from this physiological point of view, is it proper that those whose occupations during the week are sedentary, and who need air and exercise, should take just the same way of observing the rest-day, as those who have pursued an entirely different course during the week? It seems not so to me.

It seems to me, moreover, that this physiological law is not exactly obeyed in another point. There is not a proper adaptation of the modes of observing the Sabbath to the wants of any of these several classes. Take a man whose occupation is bodily exertion. The best way to recover the tone of bodily vigor is to take gentle exercise on the day of rest, as any of you who have tried it know by experience. If a man, worn out by excessive toil one day, lies entirely still the next day, on the third day he will have less vigor, less elasticity, less buoyancy of spirits, than if he had spent the intermediate day, or a portion of it, in some gentle exercise. Suppose you take a long walk, of perhaps thirty or forty miles in a day, and not being accustomed to such exercise, you feel very much fatigued and worn out. When the morning comes following your excessive labor, if you sit still all that day, your stiffness stays with you; but if you move about occasionally, if you take gentle exercise, if you go out into the fields, and especially if you combine with your exercise something to refresh the mind and exhilarate the spirits, as pleasant intercourse with your friends, and conversation on cheerful subjects, or if you devote your rest to reading books adapted at once to amuse and to instruct, blending the useful with the pleasant, you will be far more refreshed and invigorated, than if you should give up all the hours of the day to rest, and employ your mind entirely upon grave and serious subjects.

So, too, with those who are employed all the week with such subjects. It would seem as if it would be better for them to relax a little. If they must have a seventh-day Sabbath or rest, it would be better to take miscellaneous topics for discourse, such subjects as would not require very intense application of the mind, very deep or profound seriousness, but to employ their minds with something bright in the sunlight of joy and cheerfulness. Not that I mean to intimate, that cheerfulness is inconsistent with seriousness; for the depth of seriousness is perfectly consistent with the state of mind which sometimes indulges in mirthfulness, or in what the ascetic would call levity; but the highest rest would be found in permitting that state of mind to reveal its *various* modes of action at different times. Is there any harm in cheerful conversation, in pleasantry, in innocent jest, or in lively wit? Whatsoever of this nature 's proper upon any day of the week, in a physiological point of view, certainly there is no harm in doing on the first day of the week. That man, whose professional calling requires him to be mainly conversant with religious matters, should be permitted to turn away his mind from the continual intense application of its powers, to those higher and more solemn topics, and seek relaxation in pleasant social intercourse, in conversation spiced with good-natured wit and humor, and a playfulness of manner calculated to unbend the mind, and to relax the soul too closely applied to its regular pursuits during the week.

Indeed, I believe this was the idea with the Jewish Sabbath —it was a time of relaxation. I am not sure there was anything in it forbidding pleasant conversation, light thoughts, or light words; that there was anything in it which would prevent their mingling together in all the freedom and hilarity which characterized the innocent assembling of cheerful spirits on any other day of the week. Now our Sabbatical law forbids all this. It says, to be sure, that you may be pleasant and agreeable, but you must keep your mind on solemn and serious topics all the time. I know that many of those who advocate the Sabbatical observance are giving way very much, and are admitting a great deal more readily than they did, the pleasant smile and the cheerful heart. But even now, there are those who gravely exhort their hearers, as in a case which has been alluded to here, if they meet a friend or a stranger, to pass him without a word; if they are addressed, not to return the salutation. If that is the strictness of some even now, we can easily see what must be the sentiments which uphold the doctrine of such a mode of observance, and what must have been the condition of the country when that spirit prevailed throughout all the borders of the land. Such was once the spirit of all our religious teachers; and if men now profess a different temper of mind, it is not owing to the Sabbatical observers and their labers, but, on the contrary, it is in consequence of widely spread liberal views; it is in consequence of the labors of " heretics," of " infidels," and " Sabbath-breakers;" it is in consequence of the labors of such men as these, that the jail-keepers are obliged to shove the shutters aside, a little way, and allow a few more gleams of the sunlight of joy to peep in at the grated windows, than were formerly allowed. We ask that the prison-door be thrown open, that the iron grates should be torn from the windows; and the same influence which has relaxed it somewhat, will keep it relaxing more and more, until by and by there will not be rigidity e ough in the material to keep the latch upon its staple; and thus we shall accomplish what we aim at, and make the Sabbath practically, what it has long been declared to be, an institution for man, and not superior to him.

The theory of the Sabbath, which is upheld by the strictest defenders of it, still enjoins just as much avoidan e of all innocent cheerfulness, as the theory and practice together enjoined in older times. Now where is the physiological law in favor of that? These are our opinions, that, even admitting the seventh part to be the proper proportion of the time for rest—even admitting that the twenty-four hour period is the proper division—we object that there is not a due discrimination between the different classes, callings, and conditions of men, adapting the day of rest to the needs and wants of each man, according to his condition and circumstances; that there is not even a fitness in those employments to any of those classes.

Again, we object on the physiological ground to the given

law of division, giving us twenty-four hours out of a hundred and sixty-eight to rest, and leaving a hundred and forty-four to bodily toil, at least as many of them as you can possibly crowd into the season of labor—fifteen, twelve, or ten hours per day, whichever it may be. We believe a different distribution is better than that. Let the amount of time to be devoted to bodily toil be what it may; let the amount to be devoted to rest be what it may; let the amount to be devoted to intellectual, moral and religious instruction be what it may; still it is better, we believe, to divide those hours over the whole seven days of the week, than to put all of one class into six days, and all of the other class into one day. For example—if we believe ten hours a day should be devoted to bodily toil, which I believe is quite as much as we should devote to it; that is, ten hours a day during six days in the week; it would be better to take the sixty hours, and divide them into seven portions, than to divide them into six. You thus secure out of every one of the ten hour periods, a sixth-part of the ten hours to be added to the rest-season, which is better than to leave the ten hours entire for labor, and then to have one day without any labor in it. We want some kind of exercise every day, in order to be healthy. We believe that if a man sets himself down in the parlor as soon as he is up in the morning, and sits as still as possible until meeting-time, and then walks a few squares or half a mile, or rides perhaps to meeting, and as soon as meeting is over, goes home and sits still till bed time, will feel a great degree of langour, depression, and want of elasticity, and will find himself almost as much fatigued, and spent, and worn out with his day's employment, as with the preceding day's manual labor.

I have some experience upon this subject, having been brought up "after the most straightest sect of our religion," upon this point—having been taught by teachers and parents, and sincerely taught, that the first day of the week was holy. When the last ray of the sun-light faded from the hill-tops on Saturday night, no matter how eager I might be in my play, or in the pursuit of some childish avocation, however absorbed

my youthful mind in study, or in anything else, even to enthu-
siasm, when the faint light on the tree-tops disappeared, I was
taught to lay aside the plaything, or the slate-pencil, or the
book—to lay aside everything, and sit down in the quiet,
through that evening and the next day, sometimes to read the
Bible, and sometimes to read some theological book—for I
remember that then it was a relief to take down a huge book
of didactic theology, and pore over it, hour after hour; it was an
escape from the tedium of doing nothing. Judge for yourselves how great was the evil that I was trying to escape from.
I do not know how far the experience of others compares with
my own upon this point, but the moment the hours of the Sabbath were over, I was eager to join the companionship of my
friends and play-fellows in the street with the hoop or the ball,
and there was no time during the whole week when the play
was more loud than on the first day of the week, where I was
brought up. We were racing off the load and weariness of the
Sabbath burden. As I grew older, and became fatigued with
the prosecution of the toils of the week, then indeed Sabbath
morning was greeted with pleasure; but before the Sabbath
evening came, we were generally quite as willing that it should
pass away. That is the testimony, I believe, of the experience
of the great mass of the people; for I don't believe that I was
peculiar in this matter, and I know I was not peculiar, if I
compare myself with my own mates of those days; and I believe I had quite as much respect and inward feeling of delight
in regard to the Sabbath, as the majority of those who are
trained to observe it.

Here, then, is the testimony upon the physiological bearings
of the question. Twenty-four consecutive hours of rest are too
much for us. It is like overloading the stomach by eating two
meals at once, or like passing one day without food, and eating
a double allowance on the next day. You will be worse off
the third day, than if you had divided the food between the
two days with an equal distribution. Now, if we can carry out
the principle pointed out, we shall find a more excellent way.
We should set apart a portion of every day for the pursuit of

useful knowledge, the cultivation of the moral faculties, and for meditation on religious topics, the three ends of human meditation, and thus a part of every day would be what now the Sabbatarian contends that the first day of the week ought to be in a measure exclusively.

I know it is said, sometimes, that if we do not attach a peculiar sacredness to a peculiar portion of time, men will wholly neglect such employments, overwork themselves, and not take rest enough to repair the waste of their strength. If they do, it will only be what they do now. They violate the physiological laws in this respect now, as I have shown you; and let me give you another proof. In the cities of Philadelphia and New York, where I have spent some time, if there is one day of the week which is peculiarly marked with immorality, with gross vice, with drunkenness, blackguardism and ruffianism, it is the first day of the week. If you want to see the low grog-shops thronged, the loungers in the gathering places of sin and vice, go to them on the first day of the week. And why? Because then, the burden of having nothing to do rests upon these men. Were they to work on a part of that day, it would be different; because then the remaining part of the day would not be wearisome to them. They might retire to the quiet of their own habitations, and would not need the exhilaration of the wine-cup, or the brandy-bottle, to fill up the blank left, especially in the uncultivated mind, by the shutting out of the ordinary occupations entirely from one whole day. These gatherings in the dens of vice are so many testimonies to the falsehood of the institution that has assembled them there. We have somewhat more rigid laws against the selling of intoxicating liquors on that day than on other days. Men in favor of licensing the abominable traffic in ardent spirit, — in favor of saying that, by paying so much money into the treasury, men shall have the privilege of plundering their neighbors, and administering to their depraved appetites and passions, for six days in the week, are yet willing to forbid the sale of strong drink on the seventh. That is not more from a desire to mark the day as sacred, than it is from the conviction that, on that day, there is most need of restraint. Men are most likely on that day to give way to indulgence, and I need not multiply further proofs.

My view is, that if a few hours of every day were to be separated from the day's work, and the time were to be devoted to reading, to pleasant conversation, to moral and religious instruction, men would not be tired by the occupations of the season of labor; and a just distribution of the time would preserve a more even balance in the character. More time would be absolutely gained; the temptations which lure men to vice would be fewer; and the power of resistance to those temptations would be greater. The change, therefore, instead of tending to demoralize the character of the people, would have the most salutary moral tendency.

These, then, are the views which present themselves to me as I stand before you here, in regard to the physiological bearings of the question of keeping the first day of the week, or any one day of the week, as peculiarly holy time. I am glad that, whether from the spiritual light upon the subject, or from some other cause, the rigidness of Sabbath-observing is relaxing. I find it much more common for people to walk out, to ramble among the hills without a Bible in the pocket, than it once was. It is more common to step into a neighbor's house, and make a social call. Once, I would no more have done it than I would have jumped into the mill-pond, without the intention of coming out again.

I remember very well, that I once yielded to temptation, and accepted an invitation from a friend to spend a little while in his room. There was no improper conversation there, nor anything which would not have been perfectly proper on any other day of the week. But I was very uneasy. I did not like to say to him that I did not wish to go, because I believed it to be wrong to go upon that day; I was conscientious enough, but was not bold enough. So I thought to myself, that I would not say anything wicked while I was there; I would try to behave very properly, and to shape my remarks in such a manner as to avoid whatever was unfit for the time. My bearing was such, indeed, as to excite the observation of my companion, and he wanted to know what was the matter with me. I seized the first opportunity to return home, but it was some time before I got over the sting of conscience for doing that wrong act. I did wrong, because I went against my belief. I did just as wrong then, as I should now do by giving my testimony for the sacredness of the day. I felt accused by my conscience, and I deserved the punishment.

This shows you what the doctrine is, that was taught in those days. Even that conversation, which was serious in its character, but not technically religious, was forbidden then; and I believe that those who are familiar with it will agree with me in the testimony I here bear, in regard to the character of that observance. Now, it looks to me as if this was to stifle the soul of man; as if it was damming up the nervous fluid to prevent its circulation; and could not produce healthy results. A relaxation from the old system is going on. Men can sit down, and talk of the news of the day, and perhaps pleasantly and quietly speak upon politics, or matters which even give a play to the heat of fancy, sometimes with the interchange of harmless good-natured jests; and these things show that, for some reason, the people are becoming weary of the old Sabbatical observance, and that the physiological law is beginning to vindicate itself, in spite of the old theological systems of creed-makers.

Henry C. Wright next addressed the Convention, as follows:—

There are but a few minutes to the time appointed to take up the resolutions; but I wish to direct your attention briefly to two or three points. One is this. Our Sabbatarian friends talk much of the comparative results of the Sabbatarian and the Anti-Sabbatarian principle. The Sabbatarian principle is the consecration of one day in seven especially to God; the Anti-Sabbatarian principle is the consecration of all days especially to God; or, in other words, to consecrate man to God, every day alike. They seek to draw a distinction and contrast between the results of these principles; and refer us to drunkenness, thefts, and robberies, to the French revolution, to anarchy, and to all the evils that afflict this world, as the result of the Anti-Sabbath principle, or the desecration of the Sabbath, as they call it. My answer is this—and I believe that every man who takes the trouble to ask the question, and to investigate it for himself, will come to the same result. Who are these men that perpetrate all these crimes? They are the very men who have been educated under the influence of a Sabbatizing clergy, all over Christendom! The drunkards, the adulterers, the thieves, the robbers, the French revolutionists,* and the authors of all the violence and all the wickedness in Christendom, are generally men who believe in the Sabbatarian principle, and who have been educated under the influence of that principle. I would have our principle responsible for its own results; but do not let the Sabbatarian charge upon us the results of his own principles. I cannot go into this argument, for there is not time; but I will state the question at issue.

I hold in my hands a document of the American and Foreign Sabbath Union. They say but little of the Divine authority of the Sabbath. They base it on the ground of an express command, but they never show us that command. In the second place, they base its observance on the right of the laborer to one day in seven as a day of rest. We have no issue at all with them on that point. We admit the right and necessity of rest from labor; and as circumstances now are, we say of the first day, as a day of rest, that we believe it to be a good institution, but merely a *human* one. Let them extol, as much as they please, the advantages of a day of rest; but what we meet them upon is this—when they attempt to back up their day of rest with divine authority, and urge it upon us as a sin, if we do not keep it.

One thing more, to which I alluded in the morning. Almost invariably in their documents, when they say that God set apart the Sabbath as a day of rest, they add to it—as a day of rest and "*religious worship*," or "*religious devotion*," or "*religious exercises*." I believe the assertion, in the first place, to be

* This refers to the revolution in 1792, and not that in 1848.

utterly false. They teach to the world a lie, when they say that God set apart one day in seven as a day for religious worship. There is no such thing in the Bible, and we ask our opponents to show the passage. Put your finger upon the place. Our principle is, that we should worship God on *all* days alike, in all our occupations, whatever they may be. Our Sabbatarian friends would confine their ideas of religious worship to something to be done up in a given time and place. They *begin* the worship of God, and *end* it, on the Sabbath. And what do they worship all the rest of the week? I wish to push our Sabbatarian friends to that point, and let them answer it. If you want the Sabbath for religious exercises, what kind of exercises will you have on the other days of the week? Irreligious? They make a distinction between secular and religious employments. Where do they get the distinction? They make it solely as a matter of convenience to themselves; there is no such distinction in the Bible; God never made it. Whatever it is right to do, we should do as a matter of religious worship. I believe we may just as truly worship God by ploughing the field, reaping the grain, or doing anything which it is right to do, as in praying and singing and preaching, and infinitely more so than in the kind of praying and preaching and singing which are done now-a-days.

One word more. The Sabbatarians say that it is an immorality to run a railway-car upon the Sabbath; that it is an immorality to open a shop, to write, post, or carry letters, or to ride out for pleasure, on the Sabbath; but you may ride to meeting as far as you please, and keep your servants standing outside the door until you go through your worship, and there is no immorality about that. Our Sabbatarian friends have a queer way of settling the right and wrong of actions. If you want to know whether it is right to walk out, and take the air upon Boston Common, look at the clock! If the finger points to a particular hour, it is very sinful; if it points to another hour, it is perfectly right! If you want to know whether it is right to read a newspaper, or write a letter, to post a letter, or to carry a letter, ask, not whether the act is right or wrong:

10*

but ask, what time of day it is, and what day of the week it is! Consult the calendar and the clock. If you want to know whether it is right to sell rum, you consult the calendar and the clock; when you should look after the character and nature of the act, and not into the nature of the day, nor the name of the day on which the act is performed. These views of the Sabbath are settled in almost every man's mind, all over the country. Go into almost any family, and they have all the old phraseology stamped into their minds, and cannot get it out. The child takes his ball to go out and play. "My son," says the mother, "you must not go out with your ball to-day." "Why, mother?" "It is Sunday." "May I walk out, and take the air—for I am wearied?" "No, my son, it is God's day—it is the Lord's day." "But, mother," says the child, "whose day is to-morrow? Whose days are the rest of the week?" Can you answer the child? Are they the devil's days? The people act as if they thought they were.

Furthermore—if you want to know whether it is right to fight battles, look at the clock and the calendar. No, they do not look at the clock or the calendar, to see whether it is right to butcher men; no, that is right at all times, and on all days. The blood-stained clergy never say it would be very wicked to butcher a man, because it is Sunday. It would be very wrong to cut the throat of a pig on Sunday, but they may cut the throats of hundreds of Mexicans, and knock out their brains by the thousand, and your Boston Recorders, your New England Puritans, and your Vermont Chronicles say it is all right. The orthodox and the heterodox clergy of the country say that it is all right; for, in this, Pilate and Herod are agreed.

The hour having arrived, the resolutions offered by Mr. Garrison were read by him, and separately adopted by a nearly unanimous vote.

The resolutions offered by John W. Browne and Charles K. Whipple were also adopted.

Elizur Wright came forward, and said:—

MR. CHAIRMAN—I agree with the New Testament doctrine, that all days are alike. I also agree with the geographical doctrine, that there is no difference between days. For if one man goes round this earth eastward, and another goes westward, and they meet upon an island, one is keeping one day for the Sabbath, and the other is keeping another day; and I ask any Philadelphia lawyer to resolve the puzzle, which day is the Sabbath? I cannot see any difference. One of them will be keeping Monday, and the other Saturday, for all that I know.

One of these resolutions refers to the Sabbath Union, and requests them to prove certain propositions from the Scriptures. Now, Mr. Chairman, I don't care what propositions can be proved from the Scriptures. Almost anything can be proved from the Scriptures. That is a book I reverence as much as I ever did—more truly than I ever did, because I think I understand it better than I ever did.

This opposition to the Sabbath, I call a pro-Sabbath business, and a building up of religion. God forbid that I should stand here, or anywhere else, to depress the highest of all the human faculties, the principle of reverence for that which is above us. It is a thing which we most lack in this world.

Everything which takes away pretence, sham, outside, and the semblance of religion, — that gives religion the power to grow; that it is which gives religion the power to germinate and to grow up into perfect strength, to govern the human character. To use a homely illustration, I recollect that, in college, the young men who boarded in commons were in the habit of taking the molasses bottles off the tables in the evening, to make candy in their rooms. The government could not put a stop to it, and the reason was, that those students wore *cloaks*. Now, if you can establish the cloak of religion all over the community, you will have very little of the substance of it. Nothing so discourages real religion, real reverence, as the facility with which men can get the appearance of it. Now, there is no one thing in which there is so great a facility of getting the appearance of religion, as in Sabbath-keeping. We begin by bringing in the smallest children, every Sunday night, to say the catechism, and make them very still and very "holy." Here is planted the *appearance* of religion, for I defy any one to find in the Assembly's Catechism the *substance* of religion. There is so much there abhorrent to real religion, poisonous as the verdure of the Bohon Upas, that religion cannot grow there. But the teaching of the catechism and this Sunday observance cultivates the outside of religion; and when the man goes abroad in life, he finds that the outside of religion answers a very good purpose, and for that reason he neglects the inside of it. If you cultivate the real grain, the outside will be there, of course; but if you care only for the outside, it will be all you will be likely to get.

I object altogether to having anything to do with the Bible as the authority for the observance of this day. I don't care how much you prove that there is a Sabbath in the Bible. I have not any question, that there is a very severe one in the Old Testament, and that the New Testament saints paid a great deal more regard to it than they ought to have done, and were condemned for it by Paul himself. I think, therefore, we ought to come down to the commandments of God, written upon our hearts and natures, and there prove what it is we want.

Allow me to refer to a memorial lately presented to the Senate of this Commonwealth, and reported on, in regard to this matter. I think it furnishes great encouragement for us to labor.

———

To the Honorable Senate and House of Representatives of the Commonwealth of Massachusetts.

Whereas, the Sabbath is an institution of God, and its strict observance is the duty and the interest of a Christian people, as *corporations* as well as *individuals:*

Therefore, we the undersigned, citizens of this Commonwealth, would respectfully petition your honorable bodies, that, in all the charters which shall be granted by you for railroads, a clause may be inserted, *making all running of cars and locomotives on such railroads on the Lord's day to involve a forfeiture of charter.*

And your petitioners will ever pray, &c.

STETSON RAYMOND,	ENOCH SANFORD,
CONSTANTINE BLODGETT,	CHAS. T. GROSVENOR,
ERASTUS MALTBY,	MORTIMER BLAKE,
W. BARROWS, JR.,	GEORGE DENHAM.

In Senate, March 16, 1848.

The Joint Standing Committee on Railways and Canals,

REPORT:

The Committee believe, that the manner in which the Lord's day is used, affects the character of a people.   Where Sunday is made a day of rest from the accustomed physical and mental labor of other days, and is devoted to religious worship, and to spiritual, moral, and social improvement, outward prosperity will be seen to be greater, and the general condition and habits of individuals higher and purer, than elsewhere.   *Every man has a right to this day for his own rest and cultivation.*

In the opinion of the Committee, it is wiser to leave this great principle to work its way through the public mind, and thus control customs and conduct, than to attempt to enforce the observance of Sunday, as a day of rest, by legal penalties.

If any man chooses to disregard his right to the day, let him be careful lest he infringe upon the rights of his wiser brother; but let him not be punished for that which he regards himself alone.

Within the last few years, it is believed that the consideration of this principle has made Sunday more extensively cherished, as a blessing, than it was formerly; and that no legislation can be devised, which will tend so safely, prudently, and surely, towards a universal observance of the day, as to leave the matter where it is.

If the prayer of these petitioners were granted, circumstances are very likely to occur, where such a "clause" as they ask for would work a wrong which they would be the last men in the world to desire.   It would be very difficult to devise any prohibitory law, which would not be liable to grave objections. The Committee are not without the hope, and somewhat confident expectation, that the time will come soon, when cars and engines will not be driven on Sunday over any railroad in Massachusetts, unless for works of necessity or mercy; but they are unanimously of opinion, that legislation on the subject is inexpedient, and that the petitioners have leave to withdraw their petition.

For the Committee,

A. D. FOSTER.

I say it is a work of "necessity and mercy" to run steamboats and cars upon the Sabbath, to carry the people out of the city into the country, where they can worship God in the fields. We mean to hold on to this sentiment, and hold them to it.

We ask them not to run cars to traffic in, but cars to meet the necessity of human nature, and the mercy we ought to show to those who are used up in traffic on the other six days of the week. It has been remarked, of late, that in the city of London, there is less disease and less mortality than there used to be. I recollect very well, that a member of Parliament remarked to the Committee who were considering the subject of running Sunday trains, that they would increase the health of London. I have not the least doubt of it. The city of London is greater than Boston, but perhaps it is not greater than Boston will be; and I am sure, from the looks of our population, that there is a necessity that they should visit the country. So far as the railroad companies are concerned, it should obviously be a work of *mercy*. They should not exact a profit; they should run the trains at cost, that every poor washerwoman with her child may be able to take a trip across the country, and be thus placed in a situation to use the other six days more to the glory of God, and to the good of herself and her fellow-men, than ever before. What is the Sabbath-rest? Now, I agree with the statesman, whom my friend Garrison quoted; I do not believe it is a curse to eat bread by the sweat of the brow; but I believe it is a curse to sweat, and not eat the bread. I say, a day of rest is wanted for those who toil, sitting still, taking stitches, or driving pegs, in the same attitude, day after day. It is no rest to them to be pent up in church pews, breathing over the atmosphere of hundreds of other people, all of them in part in a state of decay,—breathing poison. That is not what the shoemaker or the seamstress wants; not a bit of it. It is no rest to them—it is labor—and taking into view a dull sermon, pretty hard labor too.

On motion of Mr. Garrison,

Voted, That the officers of this Convention be a Committee to prepare a memorial for the repeal of all laws relating to the observance of the Sabbath, to be circulated through the Commonwealth for signatures, and presented at the next session of the Legislature.

Adjourned to meet at 7 o'clock.

Evening Session.

Convention met pursuant to adjournment, the President in the chair.

Rev. Samuel May, Jr., addressed the Convention as follows:—

I have desired, Mr. President, at several times since this Convention commenced its sittings, to obtain an opportunity to say a few words on the great subject which has called us together. It may be, indeed, of very little consequence to the Convention, what my opinions are, or whether I express them here or not. But, to myself, it is of great importance that I do not even *seem* to shrink from the position which I took as one of the callers of this Convention,—that I do not seem to shrink from standing openly in the community as a defender of the inquiry and investigation which have been set on foot in this community. I wish, too, to express my sincere respect for and confidence in those persons, who were chiefly instrumental in calling this body together,—those with whom the idea originated ; to express my confidence in the uprightness of their motives, in their sincere Christian desire to promote those great interests which God will approve, and by which mankind will be benefitted.

I wish to say, also, Sir, that the chief reason which induced me first to take a part in the calling of the Convention was, so to speak, a *practical* one. It may be a defect of my mind and organization, that I cannot take much pleasure or satisfaction in theorizing or speculating upon abstract questions. If any institution or custom of society seems to me to be working well, I feel little inclination to search too curiously its source and reason. If it works badly, and I am convinced it is working badly, and for the injury of man, that is cause enough with me, whatever may be alleged in favor of the custom, for setting it aside.

I have been for some years, Sir, deeply interested in the Anti-Slavery question. As I have of late gone from place to

place, speaking upon this subject,—and previously also, while
in the ministry in Worcester county,—I have perceived that
it was much more difficult to get the ear of the people at
large, in order to lay before them the story of the wrongs and
sufferings of their enslaved countrymen, on the first day of
the week, than on any other. I found that, by a very great
majority of those who called themselves Christian ministers,
and Christian churches, the claims of the slave were almost,
and in some cases altogether shut out, on what they call the
Sabbath. Here then I found a state of things, where the popular idea and use of the Sabbath were working very badly,
working against true religion, working against Christianity. I
see, then, that the great majority of the clergy and churches of
our land are doing what they can to make Sunday, instead of
the best, the *worst* day of the week, the very worst day of the
seven,—the day which the wronged and suffering man would
pronounce most inimical to his temporal and eternal well-
being. On that day, when those who profess to be the ministers of Christ, stand up in his name to teach the people, his
voice cannot reach, through them, the ears of the people. He
said, " The Spirit of the Lord is upon me, because he hath
sent me to heal the broken-hearted, to preach deliverance to
the captive, and to set at liberty them that are bruised ;" but
those, claiming to be his ministers, will not allow this voice of
his to speak, through them, on that day. The cries of three
millions of wronged and outraged men and women in this
land, those very cries which go into the ear of the Lord of
Sabaoth, upon the first day of the week, equally as on every
other day, are not suffered on that day to reach the ears and
hearts of the people. The gospel of Christ,—Christ himself,
therefore,—to this great extent, cannot be preached upon the
first day of the week, and is not preached. That "pure religion and undefiled, before God and the Father," which consists in visiting the widow and fatherless in their affliction,
the suffering one who has no helper and no defender,—which
emphatically *consists* in doing this, as well as in keeping one's
self unspotted from the world ;—that religion, I say, is not set

forth to the people on the first day of the week, by a very great majority of those who profess to be the religious teachers of the land. It is *suppressed* on that day. There are, indeed, ministers and churches which form exceptions to this. I wish that I could except the whole Unitarian body with which I have been connected, from these charges. I wish I could say that they were, as a body, true to their professions, to their idea, and were ready to welcome all these subjects on the first day of the week. But they are not. [A voice in the audience was understood to call this in question.] I have had some experience as a preacher in the Unitarian denomination, in endeavoring to bring this subject before congregations, and I know they are *not* all ready nor willing. There are a few, comparatively very few, who will, frankly, and at some hazard to their position and interest, allow one like myself, (to whom, perhaps, many objections may lie,) to stand in their pulpits, and advocate distinctly the rights and claims of the enslaved.

I had hoped to meet many of the Unitarian ministers here to-day. The essential views which have been declared in this Convention are in harmony with those put forth, in times past, by the Unitarian body. I grew up in that body. I never was instructed from their pulpits to hold the first day of the week as the *Sabbath* of God's command. When, at a subsequent period, I entered upon the study of my profession, I did not find the Sunday held or inculcated as the *Sabbath*, but as the Lord's day, a day commemorative of the resurrection and the gospel of Jesus Christ. It certainly was a day set apart, among Unitarians, as other sects, for religious, or it may be sectarian purposes; but not as time holier in itself than any other time, nor was it called the Sabbath. And I contend that it is little better than a fraud to give the name of Sabbath, in any case, to the first day of the week. "The *seventh* day," said the Jewish law, the only law which ever established a Sabbath, "the *seventh* day is the Sabbath of the Lord thy God." What right has any man, or body of men, to alter this, and say, "The *first* day is the Sabbath of the Lord thy God"? The Seventh-day Baptists are the only consistent Sabbatarians among the Christian sects of this country. Looking into the Scriptures, both of the Old and New Testaments, they find no other day prescribed as a Sabbath, but the *seventh*, and to that they adhere, and are consistent in doing so. All others, who profess to hold sacred the authority of the Scriptures, are inconsistent with themselves, and undermine their own position, by maintaining that the first day of the week is the *Sabbath.*

But, Mr. President, as I said in the beginning, whatever theory we may adopt on this subject, let it be one which shall not conflict with the great interests and aims of the gospel of Christ. If the first be by any one substituted for the *seventh* day of the week, and held as a Sabbath, let him remember the words of Jesus, "The Sabbath was made for man," — for *humanity* in all its varying trials, temptations, woes and wrongs. No question of humanity can be excluded from the hours of Sunday, without a palpable dishonor and wrong being done to Christ and his gospel. And he who would fasten the yoke of such a Sabbath as this upon the minds and consciences of the people, ought to be regarded as among the foremost foes of God and man.

Lucretia Mott said : —

Our friend makes a difference between calling the day Sabbath, and recognizing it as the Lord's day. Is not this a distinction in terms only, but the same thing in fact ? The mere change of the day from the seventh to the first of the week, does not meet all the wants of the people on this subject. We may call it Sabbath or Lord's day, and be equally in darkness as to the nature of true worship.

We may deceive ourselves, in our care not to offend our neighbors, who are Sabbatarians, or Lord's day observers. For their sakes, we will seem to observe the day ; refraining from that which, on another day, would be right. We will not permit our children to play in the yard, or be seen ourselves doing that which would wound them. Upon a closer examination of our motives, it may be our own love of approbation and selfishness that is wounded. If so, there is a kind of hypocrisy in the act of seeming to be what we are not. We have need to guard ourselves against any compromise for the praise of man's sake.

For years after my mind was satisfied on this subject, if engaged in sewing, on the first day, and a domestic or other person entered the room, the work was concealed, with the plea that their feelings should not be hurt. But, on being asked, why I did not also, for the same reason, go to the communion table, or submit to baptism, I could not answer satisfactorily; and was at length convinced that more harm was done to myself and children, in the little deception practised, than in working "openly, uncondemned, and in secret doing nothing."

As advocates of the truth, we must be willing to be " made of no reputation," to lose caste among our people. If we seek to please men, we " make the cross of Christ (to use a symbolical expression) of no effect." Let us, therefore, stand fast in the liberty wherewith the truth has made us free.

Rev. John M. Spear said :—

For some two or three years past, sir, I have devoted very much of my time to speaking to the people in behalf of the prisoner, persuading the people not to kill him, but to spare his life,—to treat him kindly when he is released from prison, and to abolish those wretched buildings that we now call prisons, and to substitute in their place the asylum, laboring to reform and save, rather than to punish and to destroy. Going out, therefore, into various towns and villages, sometimes invited and sometimes uninvited, I have met with various obstacles in the way. Among these obstacles is the popular view of the Sabbath, that this day is too holy to labor for the criminal.

Travelling a few months ago in the neighboring State of Rhode Island, I stopped with a friend, and said that I would speak there on Sunday evening in aid of this cause. He sent notices around to all the clergymen of the place, some dozen or more. Several of the clergymen read the notices, but one would not. He, however, told the congregation that he had a notice of a meeting, but could not read it, for it

was to be held on *Sunday evening, and for a secular purpose.*
The next day after the lecture, passing round in that village,
I met with one of that clergyman's parishioners, and he expressed a very deep interest in what I was endeavoring to
do in aid of the prisoner, and assured me that he certainly
would have come to the meeting, had he known the subject
on which I intended to speak ; and then he told me that his
minister had refused to notice the meeting, because it was
for a secular purpose, and to be held on Sunday evening.
" Pray, sir," said 'I, " what was your minister's subject that
afternoon ? " " The last judgment." "A very solemn subject,
indeed ; and do you remember any Scriptures your minister
quoted, having a bearing, as he supposed, upon this last judgment ? " "The twenty-fifth chapter of Matthew." " And
what did he tell you would become of you, if you did not discharge these duties ? " " He said we should go to hell." " And
would you ever get out ? " " Never ; if we once got into that
place, there was no relief, and there was no end to it." " Then,
sir, it is vastly important that you should understand what
these duties are ; " and I repeated to him the closing part of
the chapter—" Come, ye blessed of my Father, inherit the
kingdom prepared for you from the foundation of the world ;
for I was an hungered, and ye gave me meat ; thirsty, and ye
gave me drink ; naked, and ye clothed me ; sick, and in prison,
and ye came unto me." " Here," said I, " among these duties
enjoined in the twenty-fifth chapter of Matthew that your minister quoted as having a bearing upon the last judgment, is
the duty of visiting the prisoner,—ay, and the climax of all
these duties ; and yet your minister ventured to stand up in
his pulpit yesterday, and tell you that that was a secular affair,
and so secular that he could not even read a notice of a meeting for that purpose, because it was to be held on Sunday
evening ; and so he kept his congregation away, and prevented
them from coming to an understanding of that matter." Sir,
it seemed to me that that minister was doing, by that act, very
great mischief ; and when I learned that there was to be a call

for the consideration of this great subject, I rejoiced that such
a meeting was to be held in Boston.

But, sir, there is another side to this matter. Prior to that
time, I went out into Norfolk County, and called on a good
friend, (and he is here to-day,) on a Saturday night. I told that
preacher that I wanted to speak in his pulpit on Sunday evening. "I don't want any such thing done here," he said ; "I
am decidedly opposed to it." I was surprised, and said, "I
had seen you at the anti-slavery meetings, and I thought that
perhaps you would be friendly to having such a meeting here."
" Yes, but I cannot bear the idea of having the subject put off to
a *third service,* as though it did not belong to Christianity. My
congregation is a scattered people, and will come up here to-
morrow afternoon, and that will be the time for you to spread the
subject before them." It seemed to me that there was a man
who understood the matter, and I rejoiced at it; and I never
see friend Coe, without thinking of the lesson he taught me.
When you tell me I may lecture on Saturday or on Monday
night, or on Sunday night, I ask why can't I lecture between
ten and four o'clock on that same day ? Sir, I press this
matter.

Unitarians have been spoken of by some of our friends to-
night. Sir, I honor that body. In this matter, I think they
have set a noble example. They have been more willing than
any other sect in the land to open their pulpits. I want to ap-
probate men for the good they do. I don't want to be all the
time pointing out the evils men are doing. It seems to me that
we ought, when men do good, to hold up that good, to encourage others by their example. I rejoice that these persons have
ventured to open their pulpits in this way. Why should not
friend May, friend Garrison, friend Wright, and others, speak
anywhere that the people are together to hear? Entertaining
this view, I rejoice that the meeting-house is already built for
me. I rejoice that when I arrive in a place, the people have
already laid aside their avocations. I rejoice that the congregation is already gathered for me. It seems to me that it will
save me a vast amount of time and labor. What we want,

11*

then, is to make a good use of the day. I want that we should lecture on Temperance, Freedom, Peace, and the Reform of the Criminal, on that day. I don't care, as I think my friend behind me (Mr. Foster) does, to have the people all scattered, and out in the fields. I am glad, on Sunday morning, to find the people there, and if they will let me speak, I rejoice in that gathering; but if not, I will expose the hypocrisy that will quote the twenty-fifth chapter of Matthew to prove the last judgment, and when you ask them to do a duty there enjoined, will tell you that it is secular. This idea of dividing off duties, labelling some of them "secular," and some of them "religious," has done an immense amount of mischief.

Mrs. Mott called for the reading of the resolutions offered by Theodore Parker, after which she made the following remarks:

I did not ask for the reading of these resolutions again, with the intention of speaking upon them, but that, in justice to him who presented them, they should have an intelligent hearing and understanding, and passage, if it be so judged, in this Convention.

Some of them do not appear in accordance with the resolutions already passed here; and the tendency of them, I fear, would be rather to strengthen the superstition that prevails on this subject, than to lessen it. The object of this Convention is to remove this superstition, as well as to take measures for the repeal of all penal enactments to enforce the observance of the day. So far, its course has been in accordance with its object, as published to the world. It is important that we should carry out consistently our principles and proposed measures.

Is it needful that reformers should ever express themselves in the manner in which some of these resolutions are expressed, with regard to any institutions that they believe might rightly pass away? Those who are prone to adhere to their cherished customs and forms, will not lightly yield them. The sectarian will not give up his Sabbath too soon.

The right has been sufficiently admitted, in the speeches made here, and the resolutions passed, that all who choose should voluntarily associate themselves in the observance of the day, for as long a time as it may yield them any profit. But it would be too much to ask of us, that we should propose to do anything to continue the sacredness of the day.

If we assert that, in the attempt to strengthen its observance by appeals to superstition and ignorance, more harm will accrue to the cause of pure religion than good. Do we fear that our devotion and piety will be called in question? I trust the reformers of this character will give practical evidence, in their every day life, of their allegiance to God. If their fruits shall testify to their faith, they need not fear the stigma or the opprobrium of the bigoted worshipper, because of their not holding up one day above another.

There are various reasons for keeping this Convention on very simple ground—not blending it with any of the popular views of the subject, which prevail to such an extent. We shall do more, in this way, to promote the cause of practical Christianity, than by yielding to the prevailing idea, that worship is more acceptable on one day in seven, than doing right every day of the week. The character of many of these reformers—their interest in the various concerns of humanity, the sacrifices they have made for the good of their fellow-beings—all testify to their devotion to God and humanity. They feel it incumbent upon them to be exceedingly careful in their conduct on all the days of the week, so that those who speak evil of them as evil-doers may be ashamed when they falsely accuse their good conversation in Christ. Numbers of these have seen to the end of gathering together for religious worship. They understand the vision of John in the Revelations, describing the New Jerusalem, the holy city; and he "saw *no temple* therein, for the Lord God Almighty and the Lamb are the temple of it." These cultivate the religious sentiment every day. They feel in their hearts the raising of praise and hallelujah unto their God, when they go forth into the fields and groves. God's temple is there; and they no longer need to enter the outward temple to perform their vows, and make their offerings. "Let every man be fully persuaded in his own mind."

There are signs of progress in the movements of the age. The superstitions and idols in our midst are held up to the view of the people. Enquiring minds are asking, "who shall show us any good?" These are dissatisfied with the existing forms and institutions of religious sects, and are demanding a higher righteousness — uprightness in every day life. The standard of creeds and forms must be lowered, while that of justice, peace, and love one to another, must be raised higher and higher. "The earth shall be filled with the knowledge of the glory of the Lord." We wait for no imagined millennium — no speculation or arithmetical calculation — no Bible research — to ascertain when this shall be. It only needs that the people examine for themselves — not pin their faith on ministers' sleeves, but do their own thinking, obey the truth, and be made free. The kingdom of God is nigh, even at the door. He dwelleth in your midst, though ye know it not. One of your own poets hath said —

" All mankind are one in spirit, and an instinct bears along,
Round the earth's electric circle, the swift flash of right or wrong."

This is no longer the peculiar creed of the Quaker. It is coming to be universally acknowledged in the hearts of the people, and, if faithful, the bright day of liberty, and knowledge, and truth, shall be hastened.

Many clear views have been held out before us during this Convention, to which there has been a ready response, shewing that we are ripe for advancement—that it is of more importance to live up to our convictions of right, than to subscribe to the creed of any church. May we let our light so shine, that men may see our good works, and glorify our Father in heaven, even though our worship of him may be after the way called heresy. We may be instructed by the prayer of the Apostle Paul for his brethren: "I pray to God that ye do no evil; not that we should appear approved, but that ye should do that which is honest, though we be as reprobates; for we can do nothing against the truth, but for the truth."

Is it not indicative of great progress that here, in Boston, in Puritan New England, where the Sabbath has been so long regarded with much zeal and religious devotion,—even here, there can be a large gathering of the people from day to day, and the interest continued to the end of such a Convention as this? that they can listen and bear so much? that they can receive the resolutions read here, and passed almost unanimously? I rejoice herein; yea, and will rejoice.

Some remarks have been made, tending to discourage any appeal to the State Legislatures on this subject; we have nothing to do with "the powers that be," but must trust the subject entirely to the moral sentiment of the people. But is not the very act of petitioning an appeal, and often an effective one, to the moral sense of the people? It is sometimes only by remonstrances and petitions to the rulers and statesmen of the land, that the ear of a great portion of the people is reached; and by going from house to house to obtain signers, an opportunity presents itself to scatter truth, and to enlighten the mind.

It has been so, to a great extent, in the Anti-Slavery movement. Converts have been made in this way, who are now devoting themselves to the cause of human freedom; and by reiterated appeals to the Legislatures, much has been effected for the bondman. In Pennsylvania, every facility for recovering the fugitive, and the law by which man could be held as property for six months, were removed from the statute book, last year, by the unanimous vote of both houses of the Legislature.

The success attendant on these measures should encourage us to adopt similar modes of action on this subject. Let us go away impressed with the importance of making every effort, that will induce inquiry among the people. What is done here, will be limited in its extent; but if we carry the subject home with us, and act there, we may effect something.

The Abolitionists endeavored early to enlist the pulpit and the press in behalf of the suffering and the dumb. They organized societies, scattered tracts, and sent forth the living agent; and, behold, the whole country is aroused to the subject. May it prove a healthful agitation, resulting in proclaiming liberty throughout the land, unto all the inhabitants thereof!

In this case, may not similar measures be resorted to, with equally good effect? Every fetter which superstition and sectarian bigotry have imposed, must be broken, before the mind of man will be free. The pulpit and the press may yet be enlisted even in this cause. There are many thinking minds. The people do not love to have their prophets prophesying so falsely as they have done; and they will demand an examination into this subject. If the reformer be faithful to his convictions, and make no compromise with the religion of the day; if he do not seem to believe that for which he has no respect; if he come not to the table of the Lord unworthily; the time will not be long, before the clergymen of the various sects will investigate this subject with other spectacles than those they have hitherto worn.

The zeal now manifested to increase the sanctity of the Sabbath, is not in accordance with the spirit of the age. In travelling through New York and Ohio, last year, I mourned the evidence of this sectarian zeal. Tracts were scattered through the length of the cars, on this subject, appealing to ignorance and credulity, and gross superstition. The judgments of Heaven, in numerous anecdotes, were stated as falling on the Sabbath-breaker. It is unworthy the age, when we have such works as Combe on the Constitution of Man, so freely circulated, as well as others, shewing the true workings of the natural laws, and their unavoidable results. We must, then, do our part to counteract these injurious influences of widespread error.

This is no new subject. I am one of the older members of this Convention. I have been familiar with these views from my early days, being accustomed to hear the remarks of the venerable Elias Hicks, who bore his testimony against all penal enactments for enforcing the observance of the Sabbath. He travelled extensively through New York and Pennsylvania, and after much observation, came to the conclusion, that crime and licentious indulgence were greatly increased by the existing arrangement of society, on this subject. He remarked for himself, that he was careful on the first day of the week, as on the fourth, not to do so much work in the morning, as would unfit him for the enjoyment of his meeting; but, after meeting, on either day, if he had a field of wheat which needed cradling, he would not hesitate to do it; and the law forbidding it on the first day was oppressive on his conscience. His view was, that there should be such regulation of time as should over-tax none with labor on any day of the week—that darkness was spread over the land half the time, when man might rest; and after such devotional exercises as he might choose for himself, he should have the advantage of innocent relaxation. A person present, opposing him, stated how he observed the day—that he wished all to be quiet—no secular business, &c. Elias replied, "I consider thee as much under the effect of superstition, as thou would be in the observance of any other of the Jewish rites."

During that discussion, impressions were made which I have ever remembered. They were strengthened, in after years, and I now feel the more prepared, by my feeble expression, to encourage those who have been pioneers in other labors of reform.

Mr. Garrison proceeded to address the assembly, as follows:

The great poet of nature, in one of his bold affirmations, has said—"'Tis conscience that makes cowards of us all." What! *all* cowards? Is there not a brave man on earth? Is there not one who can stand erect? Must every man cringe and tremble, as though the foundations of the earth were giving way, and the pillars of heaven falling? What did Shakspeare mean? Why, that it is conscience that makes cowards of all those who are in the wrong, and who know that they are in the wrong, no matter how just they may profess to regard their cause. Like the thief, they "fear each bush is an officer." Free inquiry they discourage — free discussion they shun. But the man who is in the right, who believes that he has eternal truth with him, is not the man to tremble or grow pale, whatever may happen. Though all the elements should combine together to beat upon him, though the mountains should be moved out of their places, he feels tranquil in his own soul. He does not feel any concern, neither is he at all in doubt, as to what is to be the end of all these things. Conscious rectitude makes him bold as a lion, while a living faith assures him that the truth will at last be victorious.

Now, the calling of this Convention has created much consternation in the Sabbatarian ranks. With a very few exceptions, the clergy are equally incensed and alarmed, and show by their conduct that they are conscious of occupying a false position in regard to this question of the Sabbath. They warn the people against coming to such a Convention ; they raise the cry of infidelity against it, and endeavor to crush it by an avalanche of obloquy. They exhibit all those signs of trepidation, that men have shown in every age of the world, who were consciously in the wrong. If they believed that their house was based upon solid rock, and not upon a sandy foundation, they would not fear, though all the winds of controversy were let loose upon it. If they were in the right, or believed that they were, they would court, not shrink from investigation. If they had God with them, and the Bible with them, and Nature with them, as they say that they have, to uphold the Sabbath, they would be serene in aspect, and magnanimous in spirit. Do you see it? If, on the other hand, we have neither God, the Bible, nor Nature with us, surely we ought to be dismayed at the prospect, and, like the wicked, flee when no man pursueth. Our Sabbatarian opponents have every advantage over us, except one—old traditions, venerated customs, ancient precedents, educational prejudices, religious examples, all are theirs. An overwhelming amount of the talent, wealth, and intellect of the land, is on their side. Numerically, we are as dust in the balance against them. Why, then, do they exhibit such symptoms of anger and alarm? Let them be judged out of their own mouths. Who are we, that venture to deny the duties and obligations of the weekly Sabbath, as enjoined from the pulpit—that dare to pronounce it a relic of Judaism, and therefore a fetter upon the spirit of Christianity ? They affirm that we are an insignificant body of fanatics, disorganizers, infidels, without reputation or influence, and almost beneath contempt. They boast that with them are all the dignitaries of the land, both in Church and State—all that is respectable, evangelical, and godly. Yet, how like dastards they behave! Of what tricks are they not guilty? to what subterfuges do they not resort? what calumnies do they not coin and circulate? how abusive and venomous is their spirit! And why? Simply because they are in the wrong!

Notwithstanding this vast disparity of numbers and influence—notwithstanding our opponents are so many, and we are so few—here is confidence, here repose, here the assurance of victory. And why? Because we know that, in a righteous cause, (and such we confidently believe is ours,) one shall chase a thousand, and two put ten thousand to flight. If we had to secure a vast numerical majority in the land, to carry our point; if we had to acquire as much wealth, talent and respectability as are now arrrayed against us, before we could succeed in breaking the Sabbatical yoke, the prospect would indeed be disheartening. But though Goliath be six cubits and a span in height, and armed with a coat of mail, and the staff of his spear be like a weaver's beam, yet it is only for the despised shepherd boy to go forth "in the name of the Lord of hosts," with his sling and stone, and the giant shall be brought prone to the earth, never again to rise.

Let me give a few illustrations. In this Convention, there are the friends of the temperance cause—teetotallers probably without an exception. Are they afraid to be rigidly examined, in regard to the soundness of their position? No—it is the rum-sellers and rum-drinkers, who are the excited party, and who give every indication of alarm. Here, too, are the friends of peace—of universal and everlasting peace. Do they dread or discountenance inquiry on this point? Far otherwise. It is the upholders of war—those who have all the swords, guns and spears on their side—who gnash their teeth, when the sinfulness of all wars is proclaimed. What a commotion is created in their ranks at the presence of a peace-advocating

non-resistant! Surely, the Romans are coming, to take away
their place and nation! Compare the conduct of the abolitionists with that of the slaveholders and their abettors!
Though the wealth and strength of the land are on the side of
slavery, the anti-slavery discussion is shaking both Church and
State like an earthquake. So in regard to this movement, but
to a subordinate extent. Not more averse to a free inquiry
into the nature of slavery are those who declare it to be a
patriarchal and God-ordained institution, than are the clergy
to a popular discussion of the sanctity of the first day of the
week. As slavery is " the corner-stone of our republican edi-
fice," so is the Sabbath the corner-stone of Christianity. Like
slavery, it is too venerable to be questioned—too sacred to be
discussed! And what does all this indicate? A good cause
and honest supporters of it? Let the candid judge!

I want to say a few words on the matter of rest as it affects
the laboring classes, because, as I have remarked before, it
seems to be the great aim of the clergy to ingratiate themselves
with those classes, by pretending to feel a lively interest in
their welfare. As if the clergy, in all lands, had not always
leaned to the side of tyranny, aristocracy, and monopoly! Our
Protestant clergy differ, in this respect, from no other. And
what do they represent Christianity as securing for the laboring classes? A poor respite from brute toil of only one day
in seven. Nothing more. Why, in this view, Moses was a
far more considerate and merciful lawgiver than Jesus; and
Judaism is decidedly preferable to Christianity! Let any man
examine the Mosaic code, and he will be surprised, I think, to
find that nearly one-third of the whole time of the people was
given up to rest, to abstinence from labor, through the multiplication of festivals and sacred occasions. Is there such an exemption from toil in this boasted Christian land, eighteen
hundred years after the advent of the Messiah? Are not the
masses driven from the earliest dawn of Monday to the latest
hour of Saturday, to enable them to keep body and soul
together? And is this the state of society which God has
ordained, to the end of the world? Why do not we, under

Christ and Christianity, enjoy as many rest-days as they had under Moses and Judaism? Nay, in this respect, observe the difference between Catholicism and Protestantism. The Romish church has its festivals and hallowed days, in addition to the Sunday, and thus relief is given to the severity of toil; but all that is conceded to us, as Protestants, is the rest of one day in seven, or fifty-two days out of the three hundred and sixty-five!

Such is not my estimate of Christianity. As taught by its founder, and portrayed in his life, its object is to undo the heavy burdens of suffering humanity, not to increase those burdens—to diminish the hours of toil, not to multiply them; and if it cannot do this, of what value is it to mankind? I do not believe that God has created us under this dire necessity to toil, like beasts, to sustain life. I believe it is his will that we should hold absolute mastery over time, so as to devote it mainly to intellectual and moral improvement, domestic enjoyment, and social intercourse. In a rectified state of society, it will not be necessary for our race to eat their bread in the sweat of their brow. Let us cease biting and devouring each other—let us proclaim and perpetuate peace and good-will throughout the earth—let us recognize and reverently obey the laws of our being—and the necessity of wasting toil will cease. God will work for us, by an omnipotent and omnipresent energy, operating upon the machinery of human invention. Our servants shall be water, fire, and air—whatever yet remains to be drawn from the unexplored and exhaustless storehouse of electricity,—to perform all servile labor, and the earth shall be filled with abundance for all. Every one shall sit under his own vine and fig tree, with none to molest or make him afraid. So shall men glorify God in their bodies and spirits, and by the redemption thus wrought out, cease to need one day in seven to repair the physical, moral and social injury inflicted on them by six days of beastly toil in the week.

I am gratified that the attendance upon this Convention has been of the considerate and sedate, the virtuous and upright, the philanthropic and truly Christian. I have never seen a more interesting body brought together, though we have had many a cheering gathering in this city. There has been a willingness to hear on the part of all assembled, quite remarkable in view of the unpopularity of this movement;—and what reform, at its commencement, has not been sneered at, calumniated, and denounced, by those who love to go with the multitude to do evil? Only let us abide our time. We are right, and that is everything. We are right, and therefore must be successful. It is not for us to give ourselves any concern as to this Sabbatical issue. As truly as God lives, and sanctifies not time, but his own eternity, he will vindicate our cause, and cover our traducers with confusion of face.

Let us be careful to disabuse the minds of a credulous and priest-ridden people, in regard to the false charge brought against us, that we would turn the day to evil purposes. We are represented as virtually saying to the profligate and vile, " Go and gamble on Sunday; get drunk, and be licentious; or ride your animals almost to death, to gratify your disposition for racing." The religious papers are giving to them the idea, that we design to countenance them in these wicked acts. It is a malicious and monstrous accusation. No; those who are engaged in this work are for elevating, not depressing the standard of morality. They have done something—who have done more?—for the cause of Temperance, of Peace, of Purity, of Labor; something to redeem the slaves from their fetters; something to propagate the doctrine of human brotherhood. What evil have they advocated? Of what crime have they been convicted? They are known by their fruits. I do not believe that there can be found on earth a more pure, a more unselfish, a more reformatory, a more truly Christian body. But " if the master of the house be called Beelzebub, how much more they of his household?" Now, this is my reply to the charge alluded to. They who indulge in drinking gambling and horse-racing, are not *our* disciples. They know us not, except to hate us. They do not believe in our doctrine of abstaining from all iniquity, and sanctifying all time alike. They believe what they have been taught, that the first day of

the week is the Sabbath, though they desecrate it—and this is
their highest idea of Christianity.

What sort of a syllogism is this—that because we deny the
peculiar holiness of a certain day, therefore we are for desecrating that day by immoral conduct?

Now, the people have an idea of only one day in seven to be
given to God. On Monday morning, after Sunday is past, they
absolutely look like different persons—do they not? Can you
conceive a wider contrast in their mien and behavior, than is
seen between Sunday and Monday? If a man did not well
understand this wonderful change, and should form acquaint-
ances on Sunday, he would have to be introduced again on
the next day, such entire strangers would they be to him.
When the Sunday is past, the whole community breathes as
if the night-mare had passed. They feel better; they begin to
feel natural; it was all unnatural before. There is a different
look, gait, walk, and voice. Now, we tell them that they are
deceiving themselves; that such religion is vain. May God
give us strength to consecrate our lives to the work of doing
good continually, without any regard to days, or times, or seasons; so shall we be free indeed, and thus enter into the true
rest.

Further remarks were made by Parker Pillsbury and Stephen
S. Foster—the latter dwelling mainly upon the duty of Anti-
Sabbatarians to show, in a practical manner, their disregard
of the first day of the week as holy time, by working, and, as
far as practicable, transacting their business, as on other days
—taking care, especially, not to countenance regular attendance
on what is popularly styled public worship. On Sunday, when
at home, he usually chopped his wood; and he had sometimes
wished that he resided close to the "sanctuary," so called, that
the sound of his axe might be heard by all the congregation—
not for the purpose of annoyance, but to indicate his deliverance from the Jewish yoke, and the scope of Christian liberty.
If there be no such thing as a holy day, he desired to see those
who take this ground acting in consonance with their belief.
Consistency and duty required it at their hands. But so long

12*

as they outwardly conformed to the prevailing views on this subject, they impaired the force of their verbal testimony, and helped to perpetuate a hurtful superstition.

Resolutions Nos. 4, 6, 7 and 9, offered by Theodore Parker, were, on motion of Lucretia Mott, adopted.

The following resolution, presented at the request of Dr. Daniel Mann, was adopted by acclamation :—

Resolved, That a Committee be appointed to request the different railroad companies to run Sunday trains, at low rates of fare, to afford cheap and rational recreation to, and promote the health, morality, and well-being of that class of thé city population, who are confined to toil and poverty during six days of the week.

Voted, That the officers of this Convention be a Committee to carry into effect the foregoing resolution.

Adjourned, *sine die.*

GEORGE W. BENSON, *President.*

DANIEL RICKETSON, } *Secretaries.*
ELIZA J. KENNY,   }

APPENDIX.

SPIRIT OF THE CLERGY AND THE RELIGIOUS PRESS.

The proceedings of the ANTI-SABBATH CONVENTION are faithfully recorded in the preceding pages, to which the candid and critical attention of all who are interested in the progress of the human race is solicited. They need no defence, and we believe will bear the severest scrutiny, whether relating to the spirit by which the body was animated, the object it had in view, or to the reasoning adopted on the occasion. Of the numerous "religious" journals which have noticed the Convention,—all edited by clergymen,—almost every one has resorted to ridicule, falsehood, carricature, scurrility. In order that the people may see in what manner these journals have attempted to deceive them, in regard to the character and aim of the Convention, the following extracts are appended, to which many others of a similar stamp might be added, if necessary.

[From the Boston Recorder.]

OVERTHROWING THE SABBATH.—What! asks the reader, who are thus engaged? Had he looked with us into the Melodeon on Friday last, he could easily have determined. He would have there seen the insane demonstrations that have so often been the centre of amusement and of disgrace in our city. There stood first and foremost, WILLIAM LLOYD GARRISON, the sun of the orbit which he describes. Around him revolved, as lesser luminaries, ever obedient to the law of powerful attraction, by which they are held in place, C. C. Burleigh, who, judging from his beard, has evidently long resided at Jericho, Abigail Folsom, Henry C. Wright, Theodore Parker, and others.

We happened in the time the resolutions reported by the master-spirit of the movement were under consideration. Slight, unessential modifications were proposed, but all went as he directed. He, in fact, rode upon *the whirlwind of irreligion*, that there spent itself, and made those fiery spirits but tame spaniels at his feet, say amen to "the cut and dried" *string of blasphemies*, that had been duly concocted and prepared.

But the number who voted for the adoption of these, was beggarly enough. They described a circle around the room, which was considerably filled with curious spectators, and on the passage of *each blasphemy*, the vote ranged, we should judge, somewhere between five and twenty voices, certain of the resolves calling out a stronger expression than others.

Disappointment and chagrin evidently sat upon the countenance of the leader in this movement, and that of his satellites. Their last muster at their annual winter gathering at Faneuil Hall, was contemptible enough. Maddened by the failure, *so much as to excite a mob* on that occasion, it seems likely this bold, and we hope *last push of impiety* was attempted. It seemed necessary to make capital in some way. Notoriety and billingsgate, though enjoyed amid chaos and uproar, were too sweet to be surrendered. Hence the call, as it appears, for the *Anti-Sabbath Convention*. But its most signal failure, it is hoped, will rebuke even Garrison himself—will, at all events, serve to place him where he has long deserved to stand—*the prince of New England Infidelity*. It is especially gratifying to see, that when he summons men to overthrow the institutions of the Most High, and "calls spirits from the vasty deep," they come not. We may well rejoice that the influence of such a man has at length ripened into a corruption, that is nauseous to the whole people.

The resolutions which he brought forward, and which some of the enemies of religion will no doubt industriously circulate, were of so extraordinary a character as to carry along with their bane an antidote. We suppose that with the passing away of whatever is novel in this movement, its abettors, leaving the fourth, will attack the other *nine* commandments of the decalogue. When these are all swept away, and every religious and social restraint with which society is now encompassed,—as the chieftains in this warfare seem to hope,—what a scene would ensue for depravity and hell to gloat over! Mr. Garrison was understood to remark, that "there is nothing on earth that is sacred but man!" Of course, the Bible is no infallible authority, and all Divine institutions are human inventions or fables. We wonder which of these he and the rest of his vanguard will next assault;—the family, we believe, alone remains to them as a fresh object of attack, civil goverment, the ministry, the church, and now the Sabbath, having been all abolished.

[*From the Congregational Journal,* Concord, *N. H.*]

ANTI-SABBATH CONVENTION.—It was foreign to our intention to take any notice of this out and out *Infidel* gathering in Boston ; and but for the request of others, we should not depart from our purpose. They judge that a sketch of its proceedings should be spread out in our columns as an illustration of the down-hill course of error, and the end of sham reformers and religious apostates. Thanks to Heaven! New Hampshire is purged of this vile trash; the people too well understand the men who have labored for years to break down civil and Christian institutions together; not an individual of them can beg his bread by vagabondizing to and fro through the State, and walking up and down in it in the name of a reformatory lecturer or agent; their occupation is gone; and either they must go to work like honest and industrious men, however they dislike it, or take the alternative of starvation.

Rev. Theodore Parker introduced resolutions to the effect, that though they discarded the *divine authority* of the Sabbath, yet as mankind need rest, and the social worship of God is the duty of all, there could be no harm in combining these two objects, and employing the first day of the week to secure them. These resolutions were received with great indignation, and voted down unanimously, it being maintained that the wicked priests could never be put down, so long as they could get the people together once a week to hear them, be it the Sabbath or any other day.

Mr. Garrison was the lion of the occasion; the wire-puller and fac-totum, before whom all the lesser animals quailed, and obsequiously did his bidding.

A letter was read from a female operative in a factory, opposing the abolition of the Sabbath, as in that case, she feared there would be no day of rest from crushing and exhausting toil; but the reformers did not think her objection worthy of regard, since, in fact, they are regardless of the present comfort and interests of the toiling millions, to say nothing of the future : nor merely regardless; they are the deadly foes of the laboring classes, not a few of whom have been wrecked of happiness and hope by their insane measures.

The speakers having talked till all others were tired of hearing, if the orators were not of talking, the conventicle adjourned for a year, furnishing in their own example, a most convincing argument for the Sabbath, in the absence of its appropriate influence upon themselves.

The following *jeu d' esprit* appeared in the Boston Post, containing not only satire, but sound logic :—

ANTI-MONDAY CONVENTION.—The undersigned, not believing in any day of the week, and especially opposed to Monday, regarding it as heathenish in its origin, and calculated to keep back the progress of social cleanliness, by fostering the absurd notion that people can only wash on that day, earnestly call the attention of the good people of this Commonwealth to the subject of the immediate abolition of Monday from the calendar and from creation.

A convention will be held at the Antitheon, on Saturday, April 1st, where all interested in the matter, and especially laundresses, tub-makers, and soap-boilers, are respectfully invited to attend.

> ALMOST ALLCLEAN,
> WELL-WASHED WHITEFACE, } *Committee.*
> NO SPOT OR WRINKLE,
> ANTI-SUDS NO-TUB,

[From the Christian (Universalist) Freeman.]

THE ANTI-SABBATH CONVENTION. — As we were absent from home the most of last week, we did not report to our readers the doings of this Convention. As we spoke of it in prospect, and broke a lance with the prime mover in the business, and bishop of the proposed chaos, Wm. L. Garrison, our readers will expect to see in our columns some account of the workings of the body.

Well, the Convention met, and organized. Mr. Garrison introduced a long series of resolutions, the focus of which went for the annihilation of the Sabbath, and every thing like it, either as a legal or voluntary associational religious arrangement, and every thing in the shape of a religious institution.

That we do not misunderstand the spirit of the resolutions, and the sentiment of the prime movers of the project, is evident, not only from the language of the resolutions, but their opposition to other resolutions, which were designed to save something like a voluntary religious institution. Watts, in his rules of ascertaining the meaning of an author which is disputed, says we may gain very certain information from the objections which he anticipates from his opposers. We safely conclude that a writer does not hold a view which he admits to be an opposing one, and labors to refute. Now, Rev. Theodore Parker, who, if he is not quite a stork, appeared on that occasion as a crane among storks, feeling ashamed of the rabid, anarchical sentiments of his masters in the meeting, introduced some resolutions to this purport,—that while all laws of compulsion in respect to the observance of the Sabbath should be repealed, and there should be no superstitious reverence for one day more than another; yet, the observance of Sunday as a day of rest, and of meetings for Christian culture, had been productive of much good, and should be still encouraged. But this sentiment was put down by Mr. Garrison, and his master spirits, Pillsbury, Foster, *et cetera*, and these resolutions of Mr. Parker were rejected by the meeting. Of course, if Mr. Parker will obtain a full commission of honor from this board of American Knights, he must sell himself, soul and body, to the war of extermination against every thing in the shape of social arrangement for religious culture. This, gentle reader, is no hyberpole; it is sober fact.

And now, without the least ill-will towards the men whose lost estate we deplore, our sense of duty compels us to utter it as our sober and thorough conviction, that the little clique of managers, headed by Mr. Garrison, are enlisted for the destruction of the civil and religious institutions of the land, and that opposition to slavery is a secondary concern with them:— that they are so engaged in the other work, that no sincere friend of the slave, and of the good order and happiness of the community, can work with them in the anti-slavery cause, without giving their aid to these other, and to them more important works of desolation. But no one should cease, or refuse to work for the great and true reforms of the day, Temperance, Peace, and Universal Liberty, because a few partizans are making the name of some of these reforms a hobby to Saracen movements. The better the cause, the more likely is the name of it to be prostituted to selfish and unworthy purposes. Brethren, put on the armor of Christian principle, and manly labor for the removal of intemperance, oppression and slavery, by the use of instrumentalities which shall establish and perpetuate the right, and the permanent liberty, virtue, order, and welfare of all the people. So mote it be.

[From the Boston (Universalist) Trumpet.]

ANTI-SABBATH CONVENTION. — Messrs. Garrison, H. C. Wright, Parker, Foster, and others, offshoots from the tree of

Orthodoxy, have been holding a two-days' meeting in the Melodeon, with the *real* design of destroying all reverence and all regard for the Sabbath as a day of sacred rest. On Friday afternoon, a series of resolutions were presented by Mr. Garrison, and adopted by the Convention,—if such it could be called, but very few persons present seeming to take any part in the work, save the immediate actors on the platform,—which resolutions went the whole length of denying any distinction in days, or that there was any more propriety in observing one day than another, as a day of rest.

H. C. Wright made a long speech, full of repetition,—a strange mixture of truth and falsehood, and a total misrepresentation, so far as he attempted to describe the opinions of Christians in regard to Sunday. He called up Lucretia Mott, and therein " caught a Tartar," for she opposed some of his main positions, and made him look not a little abashed.

During the entire session, there was a changing auditory of from 200 to 400 persons, coming in and going out, talking and walking about, some with their hats on, some reading newspapers, no inconsiderable part seeming to be mere curious spectators of the trago-comic scene which was going on around them. Ever and anon, the loud shrill voice of Abby Folsom would be raised, contradicting some assertion of a speaker, or denouncing some position taken; occasionally she would turn to the auditory, and warn them not to be deceived by the false positions of the speakers, and, waving her handkerchief, shout her denunciations, to the great apparent gratification of the mass of those present, who greeted her with loud applause. Wearied at length with her incessant interruptions, in the midst of one of her harangues, a motion was made and put, to adjourn to 7 1-2 o'clock, P. M.; but amidst the noise of the adjournment, was heard the still louder noise of the maniac reformer's voice: " Remember I have the floor!" Her fellow-reformers, however, regardless of their own avowed principles and their former practices, took measures to prevent her from gaining access to the hall in the evening.

The whole affair of an Anti-Sabbath Convention strikes us as a most melancholy illustration of the folly and cruelty of all measures professing to have the public good in view, which are not based on the principles of the Bible, and are not conducted in the spirit of Christianity. Here are men, professing to be the special friends of the poor, and the advocates of the oppressed, laboring with malignant energy to destroy that day of rest from servile labor which is the poor man's richest earthly boon, and without which he must be exposed to unremitting toil; and to deprive the community of the consolatory, improving and elevating influences of the Sabbath, by shutting up the places of prayer and religious instruction, and destroying all special observance of the day as a season for assembling even for moral and intellectual improvement. Such is Infidelity.

The above article we have abridged from the "Traveller," interspersing remarks of our own. One day of rest in seven is the poor man's blessing; and he who would deprive them of it cannot be their friend; or if he be, he greatly misjudges. their interests.

[From the Christian (Universalist) Messenger.]

ULTRAISTS OF THE WORST SCHOOL.—These Anti-Sabbath zealots have a reason for their course, which does not appear in their call for a Convention. They are rabid ultraists of the worst school, and have avowed their intention to ride, as one of them expressed it, rough shod over the church, the clergy, and the government. Their avowed object is the abolition of slavery; if we judge, by their labors, their real object is the destruction of the Christian religion. The Sabbath is a great aid to the church and the clergy; it is a day set apart to religion; and while men regard it as they now do, they will, on this day, assemble for divine worship. Thus the opposition to the Sabbath springs from a desire to prevent the clergy from being heard regularly by the masses; its destruction is thought necessary in order to overthrow the church and the clergy. The men who pursue this course call themselves reformers and philanthropists! [REV. OTIS A. SKINNER.]

[From the Gospel (Universalist) Banner.]

THE BOSTON ANTI-SABBATH MEETING.—The Boston papers —all but the *Liberator* and *Investigator*—agree that the late *grand* Convention held for the solemn purpose of enacting that the Sabbath should *not* be remembered, to keep it holy, any more than Tuesday, or any other day of the week, was a most ridiculous affair,—as ridiculous as a body of fanatics who have run into infidelity could well make it. The *Boston Bee* gives as humorous an account of the meeting as any of the papers.

[From the Boston Christian (Baptist) Watchman.]

THE ANTI-SABBATH CONVENTION.—Two weeks or more have passed away since this meeting was held, and although we looked in once to see what was going on, we have not thought it of sufficient importance to call for a passing notice. All that has been accomplished by it, so far as we can learn, is, to make the unamiable spirit, and the wickedness, of the movers in this silly and wicked business, more apparent than ever. It is really too insignificant to deserve notice.

[From the New York (Orthodox) Observer.]

THE SABBATH-ABOLITIONISTS. — The Boston reformers— Abby Folsom, Theodore Parker, Foster, Garrison, &c., were in session last week, on the expediency of the abolition of the Sabbath. Parker thought, on the whole, that the voluntary assembling of folks on the first day of the week, for instruction, was not amiss, but his fellow-philosophers denounced the sentiment, and felt bound to discountenance all Sunday meetings, as the only radical remedy and means of uprooting the pernicious institution! Abby appears to have taken more than her share in their deliberations, and one of her speeches finally broke up the meeting. It is not the first time that folly and presumption have been dispersed by a "confusion of tongues."

On the last day, the resolution of Garrison, going the whole length of declaring that whatever was right and proper to do on any day, it was right and proper to do on the day which, without any just authority, had been set apart as the Christian Sabbath, was adopted.

[From the Boston Christian Alliance.]

ANTI-SABBATH CONVENTION.—Theodore Parker, Abby Folsom and S. S. Foster took an active part in the proceedings. The audience varied from forty or fifty to some two or three hundred, as people had leisure and inclination to step in a minute, to witness the tragical and comical proceedings. The members of the Convention themselves could not agree. Some thought it is well to keep up some forms of religion on the Sabbath, and others alleged that they can never abolish the Sabbath, so long as the people are accustomed to meet together on that day for public worship.

Abby Folsom, perhaps the sanest of the company, took the stump in Washington street on Thursday evening, and held forth so obstreperously, that she was arrested and locked up in the watch-house. We believe the others kept so far within the bounds of decency, that they were not taken into the keeping of the police. We are mortified that our good city should be disgraced by such infidel proceedings; but it is a great consolation that the efforts of this handful of the enemies of the Sabbath are so insignificant, that they produce not the slightest perceptible impression on the public mind. It has been said that bad men sometimes act worse than Satan wishes to have them, and thereby injure his own cause. We hope the effect will be to open the eyes of the most thoughtless among us, upon the demoralizing tendencies of infidelity, and induce them to "remember the Sabbath day to keep it holy."

[From the Boston Olive Branch.]

ANTI-SABBATH CONVENTION.—Curiosity induced us to step into the Melodeon, on Thursday of last week, on account of the notice which had been previously given of an Anti-Sabbath Convention there to be held. At the time we arrived, nearly an hour after that appointed for the opening of the meeting, we found about two hundred assembled,—for the most part harmless looking individuals, evidently strangers to each other, and wonderers of what was to be done. Upon the platform was a solitary individual, with the head curiously bald—its nakedness only partially relieved by a few attenuated locks; an expansive forehead; large protruding eyes covered by a pair of gold spectacles; and a general physiognomy shrewd, sagacious, not to say *wily;*—a man, in fine, whose natural appearance would distinguish him amongst many thousands. This man was *Wm. Lloyd Garrison*—a name somewhat euphonious, we must allow, though associated with many of the wildest and most destructive schemes which radicalism or diabolism has invented. Mr. G. is the chief actor in all the various movements of the "come-out" factionists. He seems to have been the harlequin,—whether willingly or involuntarily, we cannot tell,—of every "reform" or *de*form movement for the last ten years. We must confess that he has talents and capacities which would fit him to occupy an exalted position in society, were it not for his ultraism.

On the present occasion, Mr. G. seemed to be the self-constituted spokesman and mouth-piece of the Convention. He opened the meeting, and, after its organization, proceeded to read, at the suggestion of a female in Quaker garb, the elaborate manifesto of the no-Sabbath advocates. This abounded in the usual quantity of invective against the church and the clergy, and society in general, denied *in toto* the divine authority of the Sabbath, and went for the utmost latitudinarianism of thought and action, at all times and on all occasions. The reading of several letters from Ohio followed, one of which declared that the Sabbath was "a mighty instrument in the hands of a corrupt and intolerant priesthood to forge and rivet the manacles of tyranny." Mr. Garrison now read a long string of resolutions, which, he said, were offered to the meeting by himself, on his own responsibility. We do not know whether this announcement was made on account of any jealousy on his part, of the honor which they would confer, or because he was fearful that the dose was too strong even for his semi-infidel coadjutors. These resolutions were permitted, on motion of some wag, we should suppose, to "*lay*" upon the table, (we should like to know what sort of progeny they brought forth, when the process of incubation was finished,) and were afterwards discussed by a Mr. Burleigh, or *Burlesque*, Abby Folsom, and others.

We left the hall before the close of the meeting, and are consequently unable to report further proceedings.   ‡‡

[*From the Boston Christian (Baptist) Reflector.*]

"Great Consternation."—In the central part of Boston, there is a large building, capable of holding about fifteen hundred persons, very commodious for public meetings; a place where Theodore Parker, the Transcendentalist, philosophizes on Sunday mornings, where the Handel and Haydn Society hold their concerts on Sunday evenings, and where Conventions meet on various occasions. As we were passing by it a few evenings since, we observed a group of young men at the door, and stepped in a few minutes to learn what was going on. A considerable assembly were gathered, and were listening to a speaker on the platform uttering himself with great vehemence, while he was graphically depicting the "great consternation" which had recently spread through this community, affecting both church and state, causing the clergy to become pale with fear, and professors of religion in all denominations to tremble in view of the approaching changes. We had just been pondering the events of the late revolution in France, and began to wonder whether the speaker was referring to the convulsions of that agitated country. But no! he was describing the actual condition of things at home—the public feeling of New England.

For a moment, here was a mystery. We had been engaged in conversation with many persons during the day, both in the city and out of it, and had met no one whose equanimity had been disturbed in any way, nor had we heard the least suggestion of startling intelligence. We were truly amazed, and wished to ask the question, of some knowing one, "What can the man mean?" Is the speaker insane? Have we lost our senses? Is there some awful catastrophe about to burst upon us? These questions came and went with electric speed; and ere long, we found ourselves respiring freely, when it came out that the cause of all this extreme excitement of heaven and earth was the meeting of the *Anti-Sabbath Convention! !*

We had heard before in our lifetime that "there is but a step from the sublime to the ridiculous;" and had never met an illustration of it so queer and striking.

Really, it was enough to move the springs of pity in the heart of any philanthropist, to look at Mr. Garrison and his associates on that platform. In the features of all of them, there was an aspect of benignity, blended with a sharp expression of fanaticism. These people live in a world of their own. They fancy themselves to be the prime movers of society. They give tone to public opinion. They touch the springs of social destiny. The world holds its breath, and waits with awe to listen to their oracles. They are born to be moral sovereigns, God-made kings, to root up and pull down, "to change times, statutes and laws." They have come to "create all things new." They wave over chaos the magic wand of reform. They drive the triumphal car of human progress.

In all their madness there is "method." They are like some persons in insane asylums, who imagine themselves to be kings and queens, and all their words are in consistent keeping with that pleasing dream. They ought to be treated kindly, and remembered in the prayers of good men; not that they can do much harm to others, but that their disordered souls need the balm of true Christianity. They are the victims of mental excitement and of false philosophy. Born and educated in a Christian land, they are nevertheless without a Bible, without a gospel, and their agitated hearts know not the sweet, bland rest of a Christian Sabbath. Their ideas are semi-pagan, and their spirit is alien from the elements of pure religion and of social order. Many of them are possessed of fine intellects, but somewhat crazed, just for the want of a firm regulating power,—a real faith in God's revelation. They resemble a noble ship adrift at sea without a helm. They crave excitement, and court the tossings of the storm. To them, a quiet religious Sabbath is intolerable. They are begging the railroad companies to send out their cars on Sunday at half-price, for the sake of recreation; and thus show that they belong to that class described by Paul, in his second letter to Timothy, as "high-minded, lovers of pleasure more than lovers of God." Surely, it becomes us to pity them, and to overcome their evil with good. **H.**

13*

[*From the (Episcopal) Christian Witness and Church Advocate.*]

OBSERVANCE OF THE LORD'S DAY.—It is a comfort to know, that the Law of God, which requires the religious observance of the Sabbath day, is required by our church, to be read in the hearing of all who worship in her courts, every Sunday morning. If, then, people choose to violate the fourth commandment, they cannot plead ignorance of the duty to "remember the Sabbath day, and keep it holy." Never was the propriety and the importance of this practice more evident than at the present time. A set of men have come forward in these latter times, proclaiming themselves the reformers of the age, the friends of humanity, the great advocates for the emancipation of man from the heavy bonds of oppression, by which he is bowed down to the dust; not so much by his own depravity, as by the usages and institutions of society, civil, social, and religious. Hence their great efforts have been directed, less to the change of men's hearts, than to the turning upside down the established order of society. They commenced their fanatical career, by magnifying one evil into such a vast magnitude as apparently to overlay almost every other sin; so that they denounced, not only those who hold their fellow-men in slavery, but all others who would not join with them in their wild crusade. They freely applied to men quite as honest and as harmless as themselves, the epithet of *murderer, thief,* and other terms equally vile ; not because these persons held slaves, not because they were the apologists of the system of slaveholding. No ; for they were neither ; but because they would not subscribe to their Utopian doctrines, nor aid in carrying out their insane measures. On no class did they seem more madly earnest to spit their venom, than on the ministers of the Lord Jesus Christ. No billingsgate language seemed beneath their familiar use, when speaking of the ambassadors of God. By a very easy and a very natural transition, they passed from the ministry of the church, to the church itself. They seriously undertook the quixotic task of unchurching the kingdom of Christ; and labored to show the Christian church to be anything but a holy society of faithful men, in covenant with God. Their course is progressive, for they are a restless people, most impatient of restraint; they can neither be curbed, nor will they consent to stand still. Development is their guiding star. Hence they passed readily from a condemnation of the church to a denunciation of a positive institution of God. They are now directing their weapons of destruction against the holy Sabbath. A convention of these would-be reformers was holden in this city, a week or two since, headed by Mr. Wm. L. Garrison, who, with his associates, Abigail Folsom, Theodore

Parker, Abby Kelley, Henry C. Wright, C. C. Burleigh, and others, worked hard, and talked hard, to persuade the honest-minded people of New England to regard the fourth commandment as of no binding authority; the Sabbath as a Jewish affair, and all civil law that required the observance of the Lord's day as a burden altogether too heavy to be borne by men in this land of liberty, in the nineteenth century of the Christian era.

When they have exhausted their stock of philanthropy and fire, upon this point, like the locusts of Egypt, they will, no doubt, move on, and blacken, by their presence, some other point of the horizon, and, with their vampire fangs, fasten upon some other institution of Divine ordination. They have already assaulted the civil government, and pronounced it of no authority. They have denounced the ministry, the church, and the Sabbath; what will they next assault? Scarcely anything is now left untouched, but the "*family*" as an institution of God. We see, by a cotemporary, that Mr. Garrison was understood to say, that "there is nothing on earth that is sacred but man." If this be so, then we may anticipate that this work of reform is by no means completed. Much mad havoc remains yet to be enacted. One thing is quite certain, that such barefaced INFIDELITY will not be able much longer to hide its hateful head beneath the convenient folds of a broad and ever-changing philanthropy.

[*From the Boston Recorder.*]

THE ANTI-SABBATH CONVENTION.—The loading of this gun made much more noise than the discharging of it. It was but a "quaker-gun," loaded with blank cartridge, and bursting at the first fire. At some of the sessions, there were but few spectators present; at others, the number in attendance was greater, comprising many who came, as a certain grave divine explained it, for *exercise*,—the pleasant follies of the scene producing a violent shaking of the sides, which is said to be very helpful to digestion. For our part, however, we felt more disposed to weep at the sin, than to laugh at the fun. We took our final leave of the spot, consecrated to the labors of Theodore Parker and Ethiopian Serenaders, with a deeper regard for the Sabbath than we felt before. That must be a good institution, which rallies in opposition to it only such a silly and senseless set as the greater part of those who responded to the Anti-Sabbath call.

As none were allowed to act as members of the Convention, but such as were agreed, beforehand, in the numerous and extravagant principles set forth in the "call," it was but a small body. In fact, it was only the Garrisonian faction, who make up the anti-slavery and anti-hanging meetings, made up over again under one more name. Among those who took a *very* conspicuous part in the business, were at least four who must be regarded as deranged persons; while others were perilously near the same sad condition; and others still would have been out and out crazy, had nature only furnished them with a sufficiency of brains to render them liable to such a calamity.

The ablest speaker was that Burleigh, so much more famous for what is *on* his head, than for anything *in* it. His appearance is slovenly in all respects; except that mass of flowing ringlets and frizzled beard, which is evidently dressed with the most affectionate care. Some one, alluding to those huge red curls, dangling down the reformer's breast and back, remarked that "he could never want for a mess of carrots all the year round."

The most influential speaker, whose dictates, whether opposed or not, swayed the whole course of things, was the redoubtable Garrison himself. At every turn in the business, his hand grasped the steering oar; and let his galley-slaves row with what intent they would, he guided all things at his will.

H. C. Wright was also on hand, with the air of one who affected to "boss the job," and pass himself off as master-workman. But the utmost he could do was to act as chief train-bearer to Garrison. His main peculiarity as a speaker is the heavy, straight-forward, and double bronzed impudence of his lying. And having once uttered a falsehood, he reiterates it with a tedious pertinacity, which shows that he cleaves to the mendicant's maxim, "that the glory of a lie is to stick to it!"

Another prominent spouter on the platform was Mrs. Mott. While she was speaking, we were forcibly struck with the truth of the doctrine of total depravity, as illustrated in this lady. Of graceful mien, with a pleasing and benignant aspect, and manifesting all those naturally amiable traits of character, which, in the view of many, disprove the doctrine of depravity, it was yet evident, by almost every sentence which she uttered, that her soul was rankling against the kingdom of God, and his Christ. She reminded us of the following passage in Knoxe's Historie of the Reformatioun: "John Knoxe his awn judgment being by sum of his awn familiars demanded what he thocht of the Quene; 'If their be not in hir (said he) a proud mynd, a crafty witt, and ane indurant Hairt against God and his Treuth, my judgment faileth me.'" P. 292, Edit. 1732.

But we pass from the persons to the performances. While we were present on the first day, the chief outcry was against the intolerable oppression of the Sabbath laws. Now, if there are any laws in the statute book which are a dead letter, they are those which prohibit the violation of the Sabbath. But by the way they were talked of in the Convention, one would suppose that they were enforced with a most cruel and oppressive rigor.

It had been decided, at the commencement of operations, that none should be allowed to speak in the Convention, who would not subscribe to the long and intricate creed contained in the *call*. There were some to whom this restraint of free discussion was very distasteful; and the forenoon of the second day was chiefly occupied in an attempt to rescind this rule. One speaker said, that an adversary of their cause had told him, that when the last Convention of the kind was held several years ago, free discussion was allowed, and Amos A. Phelps went in and "used them up" at such a rate, that they dared not show themselves again during his life-time. But now, to avoid a like discomfiture from some other champion of the Sabbath, they had precluded the chance of anything being said in its favor. The speaker remarked, that if the Sabbatarians could "use him up" in argument, he was willing to be "used up;" and if they would only do it handsomely, he would stay "used up."

S. S. Foster spoke forcibly on the same side; and did himself some credit by his honest consistency. Last evening, said he, I held up the Sabbath, in this house, to scorn and ridicule, to the utmost of my power. But think you I would have done this, if I had supposed that the friends of the Sabbath, who were present, were listening to me with gags in their mouths? No, never. Poor Foster, however, under the dictation of Garrison, was voted down; and meekly bowed his neck to the yoke, without further murmuring.

W. L. Garrison tried, though with a very sheepish look about the corners of his eyes, to repel the idea, that it was want of courage to meet their opponents, which caused them, on this occasion, to flinch from free discussion, of which he and his clan used to be such zealous advocates. No man that knows us, said he, with an effort to swagger the business through—no man that knows us will ever charge us with being afraid to meet our adversaries! "But one woman will, though," exclaimed the shrill pipes of Abby Folsom, whose running commentaries enlivened all the debates.

Mr. Garrison's main pretence for sewing up the lips of the friends of the Lord's Day was, that this was simply a meeting of professed and avowed Anti-Sabbath men for business, and not for discussion. They were now to *do* something. Hereafter there would be meetings for discussion in abundance. This was like the Dutch justice in Knickerbocker, who used to decide the case first, and then hear the pleas of the lawyers afterwards, so that he might not be bothered in making up his mind.

Mr. Benson, President of the Convention, took the same ground with Mr. Garrison. None must speak who could not say " Amen" to all the heresies in that long-winded call, because this is a meeting for *business*, and not for discussion. The arrant and cowardly hypocrisy of this pretence was manifest from the fact, that, throughout the two days, scarce any business was transacted or attempted. The time was almost wholly engrossed by discussions confined to one side of the subject. If the members were all agreed in the dogmas of the *call*, and had come together solely for the transaction of business, they might have made short work. All that needed to be done, was to hear that huge batch of resolutions, which Mr. Garrison drew from the capacious reservoir of his coat-pocket, as soon as the Convention was organized by the choice of officers, and to adopt them *nem. con.* Other resolutions might have been heard and adopted to the end of the chapter. But no. No one thought about business, except when it was proposed to remove the gag. Even H. C. Wright, for once in his life, was in favor of the previous question. After this, these hypocritical reformers must cease to tax their opposers, when these latter do not wish to be pestered by the ravings of mad-caps, with being afraid of free discussion.

We must not close without remarking, that notwithstanding all that was pretended, the signers of the *call* did not all understand it alike. Theodore Parker brought in a set of resolutions much milder than Mr. Garrison's, and quite different in other respects. He was for abolishing the compulsory Sabbath laws; but would retain the observance of the day as a voluntary thing, and with some relaxation as to the manner of keeping it. This proposition, however, met with no favor from the "root-and-branch" men; who declared that if thus much was conceded to the Sabbatarians, they would soon recover the full amount of their demands. Mr. Garrison told Mr. Parker that he was an Infidel, and a man; and exhorted him to own it boldly and honestly. (! !)

The whole concern broke up late on Friday evening, after one of poor Abby Folsom's tantrums, which consigned her to the watch-house. Not that she is any crazier than most of her associates: only she has less "method in her madness."

LETTERS OF APPROVAL.

To the Anti-Sabbath Convention, to be held in Boston on the 23d and 24th inst.

NEW LISBON, (Ohio,) March 12, 1848.

Feeling deeply interested in the objects of this Convention, I should have been present with you, had not the distance and other circumstances prevented me. I have long been of the opinion, that the religious observance of any particular day has never been enjoined upon Christians, or upon mankind at large, except by human enactment. I see no evidence of it in the New Testament. My reason fails to convince me, that God has commanded its observance. His works, as seen in the great volume of nature, give a very different testimony. They move on, in obedience to his mandate, through all their revolutions, without stopping to notice the observance of any particular day.

I agree with you in your Call, "that the Sabbath, as recognized and enforced, is one of the main pillars of priestcraft and superstition, and the strong hold of a merely ceremonial religion;" and the sooner this superstitious observance of it is done away, the better for true religion and the cause of humanity.

I also agree with the Call, in disclaiming any right or wish to prevent any number of persons from observing any day of the week as holy time, by such religious rites and ceremonies as they may think acceptable to God.

Again, the Call says—"We claim for ourselves, and for all mankind, the right to worship God according to the dictates of our and their own consciences." And is not this right guaranteed by the first amendment to the United States Constitution, and by the very genius of a free government? And what is more—this is one of the inalienable rights with which human governments have no right to interfere; and it may well be said, that any law which interferes with this right is vexatious and tyrannical—destructive to the rights of conscience, and a disgrace to the statute book.

I hope the Convention will be prepared to meet the question of the Sabbath fairly and fully. Give us the history of its institution—the regular advances it has made, from the incidents that occurred between Jesus and his disciples, on the first day of the week, up to its present all-powerful influence over the great mass of the religious community. The inquiring mind needs this investigation. So far as I am individually concerned, I feel but little interest in it. I am prepared to pass judgment upon it, without any reference to its origin or antiquity. From its favorable or its unfavorable influence upon the destinies of the race, I try it; and I think it is found wanting. But, for the well-being of the human race, I shall feel a deep interest in your deliberations.

I am, therefore, yours for the right,

SAMUEL MYERS.

To the Anti-Sabbath Convention in the City of Boston:—

Precluded by our distance from you, and by the necessities imposed by the circumstances surrounding us, from being present with you, and yet deeply impressed with the importance of associated and persevering efforts to reform the evils which will become the subject of your deliberations, we venture to address you a few brief thoughts, chiefly expressive of unity of opinions and purposes with you. That "the Sabbath" is a mighty engine in the hands of a corrupt and intolerant priesthood, in riveting the chains of mental thraldom upon their deluded followers, we have long believed; and that a duty devolves upon us to employ our moral influence for the overthrow of this wicked instrumentality, we clearly perceive. We hail with joy, then, the assembling of your Convention; and would rejoice were it possible for us to mingle our thoughts and our voices with yours, in its deliberations.

In the publications which we hope will emanate from them, we conceive that it will be very important to demonstrate that the resting of one day in seven, from labor, is not, and never was, a Divine institution, inasmuch as the physiological constitution of man is such that labor, exercise, on every day, is as indispensable to the well-being of the individual, as are the food and clothing, the natural products of such labor. And it is impossible to believe that the Creator of man first gave him such a constitution as we have described, and afterwards forbade, in words, obedience to those laws of our being.

That your Convention may prove more beneficial to the cause of Humanity than its most sanguine projectors have ever anticipated, is our fervent desire. Your friends,

A. BROOKE,	JANE NICHOLSON,
VALENTINE NICHOLSON,	MICAH BROWN,
CHAS. R. BROWN,	MALINDA T. JEROME,
SYLPA L. BROWNE,	C. M. BROWNE,
W. WHIPPLE,	PHEBE WHIPPLE,
ARTEMAS NICKERSON,	ELIZABETH NICKERSON,
ELIZABETH BROOKE,	MARGARET BROOKE.
SARAH BROOKE,	

Oakland, Clinton Co., Ohio, March 10, 1848.

VIEWS OF LUTHER, MELANCTHON,
CALVIN, TYNDALE, PALEY, &c.

———

In the Call for the ANTI-SABBATH CONVENTION, reference
is made to the views which were cherished by LUTHER, ME-
LANCTHON, CALVIN, and other distinguished reformers, as sub-
stantially in agreement with those embodied in the Call—to
wit, that the Sabbath was exclusively Jewish in its origin and
design, and that Christianity knows nothing of a holy day, as
distinct from other days of the week. We proceed to give
extracts in support of that declaration.

The views of Luther, Melancthon, and all the leading men
of the Reformation, in Germany, on this subject, are found in
the celebrated Augsburg Confession of Faith, drawn up by
Melancthon, and presented to the Emperor Charles V., in 1530,
at the Diet of Augsburg. It is a summary statement of the
distinctive doctrines of the Reformation. In this it is asked,

"What is then to be thought of the Lord's Day, and such
like rites used in the Church?" (We quote from an old col-
lection of Confessions of Faith, printed in 1656. The answer
is,) " That it is lawful for bishops and pastors to appoint ordinances—not that men's consciences should be bound to esteem
them necessary services, and to think that they sin when they
violate any of them. So Paul ordained that women should
cover their heads in the congregation; that the interpreters
should be heard in course or order in the Church."

"Such like ordinances (as the first day Sabbath) the churches
should keep for charity and quietness' sake, so that they offend
not one another, that all things may be done in order, and
without tumult, in the Church; but yet with this caution, that
men's consciences be not burdened, so as they should account
them as things necessary to salvation, and think they did sin
when they break any of them without offence of others; as no

man would say that a woman doth wrong, if she come abroad uncovered."

"Of this sort is the observation of the Lord's day, of Easter, of Pentecost, and such like holy days and rites; for they that think the OBSERVATION OF THE LORD'S DAY was appointed by the authority of the Church INSTEAD OF THE SABBATH, as necessary, they are greatly deceived. The Scripture requireth that the observation of the Sabbath should be more free; for it teaches that the Mosaical ceremonies are not needful after the Gospel is revealed. And yet because it was requisite to appoint a certain day, that the people might know when to come together, it seemeth that the Church did for that purpose appoint the Lord's Day; which day, for this cause, also seemed to have better pleased the Church, that in it men might have an example of Christian liberty, and might know that the *observation* neither of the Sabbath, nor ANY OTHER DAY, was of necessity."

"There are extant monstrous disputations touching the change of the Sabbath, which have sprung up from a false persuasion, that there should be worship in the Church like to the Levitical worship. They dispute about holy days, and prescribe *how far it is lawful to work in them.* What else are such disputations but snares for men's consciences?"

In subsequent editions of the same work, the sentence, "The Scripture requireth that the observation of the Sabbath should be more free," &c., was altered by Melancthon, as follows:—

"THE SCRIPTURE HAS ABROGATED THE SABBATH, teaching that all *Mosaic ceremonies* may be omitted, since the gospel has been preached."

LUTHER,

As quoted by Coleridge in his Table Talk, says of the Christian day of rest,

"Keep it holy, for its use sake, both to body and soul! But if anywhere the day is made holy for the mere day's sake— if anywhere any one sets up its observance upon a *Jewish* foundation,—then I order you to work on it, to ride on it, to dance on it, to do anything that shall reprove this encroachment on the Christian spirit and liberty."

WHATELY.

"In Cranmer's Catechism, published in 1548, viz: the first year of Edward VI., we find the following passage:—'And here note, good children, that the Jewes in the Old Testament were commanded to keep the Sabbath day, and they observed it every seventh day, called the Sabbat or Satterday. But we Christian men in the New Testament are not bound to such commandments of Moses' law concerning differences of times, days, and meats, but have liberty and freedom to use other days for our Sabbath days, therein to hear the word of God and keep an holy rest. And therefore, that this Christian liberty may be kept and maintained, we now keep no more the Sabbath on Saturday as the Jews do, but we observe the Sundays and certain other days, *as the magistrates do judge convenient*, whom in this thing we ought to obey.'

"By the authority of the *magistrate*, Cranmer evidently meant that of the *church*; the government of which would, of course, be in the hands of the civil magistrate, in such a church as our Reformers contemplated; viz: a strictly *national* church; in which each subject of the State is necessarily, as such, a member of the church, also. In fact, the notion I am contending against, seems, as far as I can collect, to have originated with the Puritans not much more than 200 years ago; and to have been for a considerable time confined to them; though it was subsequently adopted by several members of our church."

Luther and Calvin agree in recommending the Sabbath as a useful human institution, though they both deny that it is enjoined under the Christian dispensation.

It seems not unfit to add to the testimony of these eminent reformers, that of William Tyndale, the martyr, who first translated the New Testament into English. He says, in his Answer to Sir Thomas More, who espoused the cause of the Catholics,

"As for the Sabbath, we be lords of the Sabbath, and may yet change it into Monday, or any other day as we see need; or we may make every tenth day holy, if we see cause why. Neither was there any cause to change it from the Saturday, save only to put a difference between us and the Jews. Neither need we any holy day at all, if the people might be taught without it."

Calvin, in his "Institutes," so valued by his followers, says: Bk. 2, c. 8, &c.

"The fathers frequently call it a *shadowy commandment*, because it contains the external observance of the day, which was abolished with the rest of the figures at the advent of Christ."   *   *   *   *   *   *   *

"As the two latter causes, however, ought not to be numbered among the ancient shadows, but are equally suitable to all

ages; though the Sabbath IS ABROGATED, yet it is still cus-
tomary among us, to assemble on stated days for hearing the
word, for breaking the mystic bread, and for public prayers;
and also to allow servants and laborers a remission from their
labor."　＊　＊　＊　＊　＊　＊　＊

"*Christ is the true fulfilment of the Sabbath.*—Having been
'buried with him by baptism, we have been planted together
in the likeness of his death, that being partakers of his resurrection, we may walk in newness of life.' Therefore, the
apostle says, in another place, that 'the Sabbath was a *shadow
of things to come;* but THE BODY IS OF CHRIST:' that is, the
real substance of the truth which he has beautifully explained
in that passage. This is contained, *not in one day,* but IN THE
WHOLE COURSE OF OUR LIFE, till being wholly dead to ourselves, we be filled with the life of God. *Christians, therefore,
ought to depart from all superstitious observance of days.'*

"*The resurrection of the Lord is the end and consummation of
that true rest,* which was adumbrated by the ancient Sabbath:
the same day, which put an end to the shadows, admonishes
Christians not to adhere to a shadowy ceremony. Yet I do not
lay so much stress on the septenary number, that I *would advise
the Church to an invariable adherence to it;* nor will I condemn
those churches which have other solemn days for their assemblies, provided they keep at a distance from superstition. And
this will be the case, if they be only designed for the observance of discipline and well-regulated order. Let us sum up
the whole in the following manner: As the truth was delivered
to the Jews under a figure, so it is given to us without any
shadows; first, in order that, *during our whole life, we should
meditate on a perpetual rest from our own works, that the Lord may
operate within us by his Spirit;* secondly, that every man, *when-
ever he has leisure,* should diligently exercise himself in private
in pious reflections on the works of God, and also that we
should at the same time observe the legitimate order of the
church, appointed for the hearing of the word, the administra-
tion of the sacraments, and for public prayer; thirdly, that we
should not unkindly oppress those who are subject to us. Thus
vanish all the dreams of false prophets, who in past ages have
infested the people with a Jewish notion, *affirming that nothing
but the ceremonial part of this commandment* (which according to
them is the appointment of the seventh day,) has been abrogated, but that the moral part of it, that is, *the observance of one
day in seven,* still remains. But this is only changing the day
in contempt of the Jews, while they retain the same opinion
of the *holiness of the day;* for, on the same principle, the same
mysterious signification would still be attributed to particular

days, which formerly obtained among the Jews. And indeed we see what advantages have arisen from such a sentiment. For those who adhere to it far exceed the Jews in a gross, carnal, and superstitious observance of the Sabbath; so that the reproofs which we find in Isaiah, are equally as applicable to them in the present age, as to those whom the prophet reproved in his time."

Belsham, whose doctrinal views are the very antipodes of those of Calvin, which makes his agreement with him on this subject the more remarkable, in commenting on Colossians ii. 16, says:

"Nothing can be more explicit than the apostle's declaration of the entire abrogation of the Jewish Sabbath, which is plainly no more obligatory upon Christians than the institution of the passover, or the rite of circumcision. The fourth commandment, therefore, *is a precept which has no place in the Christian law, and ought never to be appealed to as an argument for a Sabbatical institution.* And it behooves those, who think the observation of a day of Sabbatical rest is of such high importance under the Christian dispensation, and who are so loud in their charges against those who deny, or who, as they call it, *profane* the Sabbath, to show what authority they have for this imposition. I see none. The old Sabbath is expressly repealed, and no new one enjoined in its stead; always, however, keeping in mind the very obvious and important distinction between the Lord's day as a *weekly religious festival,* in joyful commemoration of the resurrection of Christ, in which way it has been universally observed from the beginning; and as *a day of Sabbatical rest* from the common employments and innocent amusements of life, for which there is no precept in the New Testament, and no example in the primitive age; the practice of which was universally discountenanced in the primitive church, and which, to this day, prevails only in a small proportion of the protestant churches in Europe, and among their descendants in America.

In Justin's Dialogue with Trypho, the Jew objects to Christians that, 'pretending to excel others, they observe no Sabbaths.' Justin replies: '*The new law will have you keep a perpetual Sabbath.* You, when you have passed a day in idleness, think you are religious. The Lord our God is not pleased with such things as these. If any one is guilty of perjury or fraud, let him reform; if he be an adulterer, let him repent; and *he will then have kept the kind of Sabbath truly pleasing to God.* You see that the elements are never idle, and keep no Sabbath. There was no need of the observation of Sabbaths

14*

before Moses, neither now is there any need of them after Jesus Christ.'

As the law of the country requires suspension from labor on the Lord's day, it is the duty of subjects to obey it. But surely this Sabbatical observation of the day can never be of that high moral importance which many apprehend; otherwise Christ and his apostles would never have been so totally silent upon the subject. But will-worship was not confined to the apostolic age; and the censures passed upon those who do not *sabbatize* like others, are as loud and as bitter *now*, as they were seventeen hundred years ago. Let those, therefore, who understand their Christian emancipation, and who determine to stand fast in the liberty with which Christ has made them free, *while they sanctify every day as a Sabbath*, BY ABSTAINING FROM ALL EVIL, as advised by the Holy Martyr, encourage themselves at the same time by the exhortation of the apostle, and suffer no man to judge them with respect to the Sabbath day. Regard no man's censure, of whatever rank, or degree, or pretensions, for not receiving as of divine authority, institutions which Christ, as our sole head, who possesses all authority and power in the church, hath not required."

"The Sabbatical observation of the Lord's day is, by this learned writer, (Dr. Priestley,) and by many others, placed upon the ground of expediency ALONE. And if it be expedient, let it be observed; but in the name of all that is sacred, let not *expedients* of *human device* be substituted as *injunctions* of *divine authority*. The plain question is: whether the Sabbatical observation of the Lord's day is enjoined by divine authority? If it be, let the order be shown, and it shall be obeyed. In the New Testament, I see the Jewish Sabbath plainly abrogated; I see no Sabbatical institution appointed in its place; and I know that the primitive church explicitly disavowed any such institution. I conclude, therefore, that Christ, our only Master, saw no necessity for appointing an institution, without which, as many now think, the Christian religion could not exist. In whose judgment may we most safely confide?"

BARCLAY.

"We may not think that these days are holy, being persuaded that all days are alike in the sight of God."

"We, not seeing any ground in Scripture for it, cannot be so superstitious as to believe, that either the *Jewish Sabbath continues*, or that the *first day* of the week is the antetype thereof, or the true Christian Sabbath; which, with Calvin, we believe to have a more spiritual sense; and therefore we know *no moral obligation* by the fourth command, or elsewhere, to keep the first day of the week more than any other, or any holiness inherent in it."

(Barclay's Apology, 11th Proposition.)

DYMOND.

" The early Christians met, not on the last, but on the first day of the week. Whatever reason may be assigned as a motive for this rejection of the ancient Sabbath, I think it will tend to discountenance the observation of any day as such; for if that day did not possess perpetual sanctity, what day does possess it ? And with respect to the general tenor of the Christian Scriptures, as to the sanctity of particular days, it is, I think, manifestly adverse to the opinion that one day is obligatory rather than another."   (Dymond's Essays.)

PALEY.

" In my opinion, the transaction in the wilderness above related (Ex. xvi.), was the first actual institution of the Sabbath." " The words (Gen. ii. 2, 3,) do not assert that God then blessed and sanctified the seventh day, but that he blessed and sanctified it for that reason." " St. Paul evidently appears to have considered the Sabbath a part of the Jewish ritual, and not obligatory upon Christians as such." (Col. ii. 16, 17). " A cessation, upon that day, from labor, beyond the time of attendance upon public worship, is not intimated in any part of the New Testament; nor did Christ or his Apostles deliver, that we know of, any commands to their Disciples for a discontinuance, upon that day, of the common affairs of their professions." " The opinion that Christ and his Apostles meant to retain the duties of the Jewish Sabbath, shifting only the day from the seventh to the first, seems to prevail without sufficient reason; nor does any evidence remain in the Scripture, (of what, however, is not improbable,) that the first day of the week was thus distinguished in commemoration of our Lord's death."   (Paley's Philosophy.)

WHATELY.

" The dogma of the ' Assembly of Divines at Westminster,' that the observance of the Sabbath is part of the moral law, is to me utterly unintelligible. Yet unless we assent to this, adopting some such sense of the term ' moral' as it is difficult even to imagine, I do not see on what principle we can, consistently, admit the authority of the fourth commandment, and yet claim exception from the prohibition of certain meats, and of blood,—the right of circumcision,—or, indeed, any part of the Levitical law."   *   *   *   *   *   *   *

"In saying that there is no mention of the Lord's day in the Mosaic law, I mean, that there is not only no mention of that specific festival which Christians observe, on the *first* day of the week, in memory of our Lord's resurrection on the morning following the Jewish Sabbath, but that there is not (as has sometimes been incautiously stated) any injunction to sanctify one day in seven.

"Throughout the whole of the Old Testament, we never hear of keeping holy *some one* day in every seven, but *the* seventh day, as the day on which God 'rested from all his work.' The difference, accordingly, between the Jews and the Christians, is not a difference of *reckoning ;* which would be a matter of no importance. Our computation is the same as theirs. They, as well as we, reckon Saturday as the seventh day of the week; and they keep it holy *as* the seventh day, in memory of God's resting from the work of creation ; we keep holy the *first* day of the week, *as* the first, in memory of our Master's rising from the dead on the day after the Sabbath.

"Now, surely, it is presumptuous to say that we are at liberty to *alter* a divine command, whose authority we admit to be binding on us, on the ground that it matters not whether this day or that be set apart as a Sabbath, provided we obey the divine injunction to observe *a* Sabbath. One of the recorded offences, we should remember, of ' Jeroboam, the son of Nebat, who made Israel to sin,' was his instituting a feast unto the Lord on the 15th day of the 10th month, ' *even the day that he had devised of his own heart.*' The Samaritans, ' who worshipped they knew not what,' perhaps acted on a similar principle, when they built a Temple on mount Gerizim; though that ' was not the place which the Lord had chosen to put his name there;' and so, perhaps, did Naaman the Syrian, when he proposed to ' wash in the rivers of Damascus, and be clean,' instead of Jordan. One river is as good as another; one mountain as good as another ; one day as good as another, *except when there is a divine command which specifies one ;* and then, it is our part not to alter or question a divine command, but to consider whether it extends to us, and if it does, to obey it.

" I cannot, therefore, but think that the error was less, of those early Christians, who, conceiving the injunction relative to the Sabbath to be binding on them, obeyed it just as it was given, (provided they did not, contrary to the Apostle's injunction, Rom. xiv. 2 to 6, presume to judge their brethren who thought differently,) than of those who, admitting the eternal obligation of the precept, yet presume to alter it on the authority of tradition. Surely, if we allow that the 'tradition of the

Church' is competent to change the express commands of God, we are falling into one of the most dangerous errors of the Romanists; and this, while we loudly censure them for presuming to refuse the cup to the laity at the Lord's Supper, on the authority of their Church, though Christ said to his disciples, ' Drink ye *all* of this ; ' and for pleading tradition in behalf of saint-worship, &c.

" But in the present case, there is not even any tradition to the purpose. It is not merely that the Apostles left us no command perpetuating the observance of the Sabbath, and transferring the day from the seventh to the first: such a change certainly would have been authorized by their express injunction, and by nothing short of that; since an express divine command can be abrogated or altered only by the same power, and by the same distinct revelation, by which it was delivered. But not only is there no such Apostolic *injunction,* than which nothing less would be sufficient; there is not even any *tradition* of their having made such a change ; nay, more, it is even abundantly plain, that they made *no* such a change. There are, indeed, sufficiently plain marks of the early Christians having observed the Lord's day as a religious festival, even from the very resurrection, (John xx. 19, 26, Acts xx. 7, 1 Cor. xvi. 2, Rev. i. 10); but, so far were they from *substituting* this for the Jewish Sabbath, that all of them who were *Jews* actually continued, themselves, to observe, not only the Mosaic Sabbath, but the whole of the Levitical law; while to the *Gentile* converts they said, ' Let no man judge you in meat, or in drink, or in respect of an holy day, or of the new moon, or of the *Sabbath day*; which are a shadow of things to come ; but the body is Christ.' " * * *

" Nor does the expression, ' *remember* the Sabbath day,' necessarily imply its having been *before* observed; but, rather, that the precept was one liable to be violated through negligence and *forgetfulness.* We often say in like manner, ' *remember* to call at such a place,' or ' remember to deliver this letter,' &c.; meaning, 'take care not to forget it.' It is not said accordingly, ' remember not to steal;' 'remember to honor your parents,' &c.; though certainly *these* precepts must have been always in force; but they are such as no one is likely to violate through forgetfulness." * * * *

" If, however, any persons are fully convinced that the precept respecting the Sabbath was given to Adam, and also conclude thence that it must bind all his posterity, they are, of course, at least equally bound by the (recorded) precept to Noah, relative to abstinence from blood. Any one who admits these obligations, and complies with them *just as they were given*, observing not the first, but the seventh day of the week as the Sabbath, is acting on a system which, though it may be erroneous, is at least intelligible and consistent. But he who acknowledges a divine command to extend to himself, ought to have an equally express divine command to sanction any *alteration* in it. Those Christians of the present day, however, who admit the obligation of the ancient Sabbath, have yet taken the liberty to change not only the *day*, but also the *mode* of observance. I believe they sometimes allege that the Jews were over scrupulous on this point, and had superadded, by their tradition, burdensome restrictions not authorized by the Mosaic law. This is true; but if we shelter ourselves under this plea,—if we admit the authority of the written law, and reject merely the pharisaical additions to it,—we are then surely bound to comply at least with the express directions that *are* written. For instance, (Exod. xxxv. 23,) 'Ye shall *kindle no fire* throughout your habitations upon the Sabbath day,' no one can pretend is a traditional precept; yet I know of no Christians who profess to observe it. Perhaps we may be told that it is a regulation not suited to our climate. That may be an additional reason, of some weight, for believing that the Jewish Sabbath was an ordinance not designed to be of universal obligation, but seems hardly sufficient, if it were of universal obligation, to authorize Christians to depart from the divinely appointed mode of observing it. I do not, however, know of any Christians who take this liberty on the plea of actual necessity, and who do comply with the precept in summer time, and in warmer countries."

"[Another reason for dwelling on the view I have taken is, the strong disposition in many Christians to satisfy their conscience by devoting to God *only* one day in seven, while the rest of their time is given up to the world, with little or no thought of religion.

"Christians need, therefore, to be often reminded that they are required not merely not to 'think their own thoughts' on one day in the week, but, as the redeemed of Christ, to 'live henceforth not unto themselves, but unto Him that died for them, and rose again;' and 'whatsoever they do, to do all to the glory of God.' Numerous early Christian Fathers, accordingly, in their commentaries on the Decalogue, describe the Jewish Sabbath as corresponding, in the analogous scheme of Christianity, not so much to the Lord's day, as to the whole life of the Christian, to his abstinence from all works that may draw off his affections from God, and to his complete dedication of himself to his service. See Athanasius, Hom. de. Sab.; Hieronymus, in Decalog.; Origen, Tract 19, in Matt.; Chrysost. Hom. 39. in Matt. xii.; Justin Martyr, Dial. cum Tryphone;

Clemens Alexandr. Strom. lib. iv.; and Augustine, *passim;* all of whom hold this language.

"I refer, however, to these and other human authorities, not as *guides* to regulate our faith and practice; for I am taught to 'call no man Master upon earth;' but merely to shew that the *novelty* which has been attributed to my views lies, in fact, on the other side.

*   *   *   *   *   *   *

In his masterly "Essays on some of the Difficulties of the Writings of St. Paul," Archbishop Whately adds—

"It cannot be denied that he (Paul) does speak, frequently and strongly, of the termination of the Mosaic law, and of the exemption of Christians from its obligations, without ever limiting and qualifying the assertion,—without even hinting at a distinction between one part which is abrogated, and another which remains in full force. It cannot be said that he had in his mind the Ceremonial law alone, and was alluding merely to the abolition of that; for in the very passages in question, he makes such allusions to *sin,* as evidently show that he had the *moral* law in his mind; as, for instance, where he says, ' The law was added because of transgressions.' 'By the law was the knowledge of sin:' with many other such expressions. And it is remarkable, that even when he seems to feel himself pressed with the mischievous practical consequences which either had been, or he is sensible might be, drawn from his doctrines, he never attempts to guard against these by limiting his original assertion;—by declaring that though part of the law was at an end, still, part continued to be binding; but he always inculcates the necessity of moral conduct on some *different* ground: For instance:—' What shall we say then? Shall we continue in sin that grace may abound? God forbid.' He does not then add that a part of the Mosaic law remains in force; but urges this consideration—' How shall we, who are dead to sin, live any longer therein? Know ye not that so many of us as were baptized into Jesus Christ, were baptized into his death? Therefore we are buried with him by baptism into death; that like as Christ was raised up from the dead by the glory of the Father, even so we also should walk in newness of life.' ' Knowing this, that our old man is crucified with him, that the body of sin might be destroyed, that henceforth we *should not serve sin.*' And such also is his tone in every passage relating to the same subject.

"Now let us adopt the obvious interpretation of the Apostle's words, and admit the entire abrogation, according to him, of the Mosaic law; concluding that it was originally designed for the Israelites alone, and that its dominion over *them* ceased when the Gospel system commenced; and we shall find that this concession does not go a step towards establishing the Antinomian conclusion, that moral conduct is not required of Christians. For it is evident that the natural distinctions of right and wrong, which conscience points out, must remain where they were. These distinctions, not having been introduced by the Mosaic law, cannot, it is evident, be overthrown by its removal; any more than the destruction of the temple at Jerusalem implied the destruction of the Mount Sion whereon it was built."

"To say, therefore, that no part of the Jewish law is binding on Christians, is very far from leaving them at liberty to disregard all moral duties. For in fact, the very definition of a *moral* duty, *implies* its universal obligation, independent of all *enactment.* The precepts respecting sacrifices, for instance, and other ceremonial observances, we call *positive* ordinances; meaning, that the things in question became *duties because they were commanded:*—the commandment to love one's neighbor as one's self, on the contrary, we call a *moral* precept, on the very ground that this was a thing *commanded because it was right.* And it is evident that what was right or wrong in itself before the law existed, must remain such after it is abrogated. Before the commandments to do no murder, and honor one's parents, had been delivered from Mount Sinai, Cain was cursed for killing his brother, and Ham for dishonoring his father; which crimes, therefore, could not cease to be such, at least, as any consequence of the abolition of that law.

"Nor need it be feared that to proclaim an exemption from the Mosaic law should leave men without any moral guide, and at a loss to distinguish right and wrong; since, after all, the light of reason is that to which every man *must* be left, in the interpretation of that very law. For Moses, it should be remembered, did not write three distinct books, one of the Ceremonial Law, one of the Civil, and a third of the Moral; nor does he hint at any such distinction. When, therefore, any one is told that a *part* of the Mosaic precepts are binding on us, viz. the *moral* ones, if he ask *which are* the Moral precepts, and how to distinguish them from the Ceremonial and the Civil, with which they are mingled, the answer must be that his conscience, if he consult it honestly, will determine that point. So far, consequently, from the moral precepts of the law being, to the Christian, necessary as a guide to his judgment in determining *what is* right and wrong, on the contrary, this moral judgment is necessary to determine what *are* the *moral* precepts of Moses."